Amy Hequembourg, PhD

Lesbian Motherho
Stories of Becoming

Pre-publication
REVIEWS,
COMMENTARIES,
EVALUATIONS . . .

"In an original contribution to contemporary theoretical and political debates over the meaning of planned lesbian motherhood, Hequembourg creatively adapts the concept of becoming from Deleuze and Guattari. Melding qualitative sociology to post-structuralist theory, this provocative book proposes a route beyond the binaries of resistance versus assimilation and sameness versus difference."

Judith Stacey, PhD
Professor of Social and Cultural
Analysis, NYU; Author,
In The Name of The Family

"*Lesbian Motherhood: Stories of Becoming* presents a new way of viewing lesbian motherhood by explaining the processes of 'becoming' a mother. This unique theoretical and analytical approach moves from understanding identities as being static and stable to understanding how they are contradictory and in constant flux. Hequembourg draws on rich ethnographic data to provide an in-depth analysis that challenges the category of lesbian mother. The author successfully questions how scholars, legal professionals, and the public view and categorize mothers. The book concludes by offering new strategies for political organizing.

This book is an essential resource for understanding key debates and issues concerning lesbian motherhood. It provides one of the most comprehensive, balanced, and nuanced explanations of assimilation and resistance, same-sex marriage, family connections, the use of reproductive technologies, child custody, and coming-out, in the literature to date. Although Hequembourg uses lesbian mothers as her subjects, the book speaks to the broadest level of sociology. The approach presented can easily be used to study how categories and identities of other subjects are formed within, and because of, hegemonic discourses. Anyone looking to understand motherhood in general should read this book."

Nancy J. Mezey, PhD
Assistant Professor of Sociology,
Sociology Program Coordinator,
Monmouth University

Lesbian Motherhood
Stories of Becoming

Lesbian Motherhood
Stories of Becoming

Amy Hequembourg, PhD

Harrington Park Press®
The Trade Division of The Haworth Press, Inc.
New York • London

For more information on this book or to order, visit
http://www.haworthpress.com/store/product.asp?sku=5922

or call 1-800-HAWORTH (800-429-6784) in the United States and Canada
or (607) 722-5857 outside the United States and Canada
or contact orders@HaworthPress.com

Published by

Harrington Park Press®, the trade division of The Haworth Press, Inc., 10 Alice Street, Binghamton, NY 13904-1580.

PUBLISHER'S NOTE

Identities and circumstances of individuals discussed in this book have been changed to protect confidentiality.

The development, preparation, and publication of this work has been undertaken with great care. However, the Publisher, employees, editors, and agents of The Haworth Press are not responsible for any errors contained herein or for consequences that may ensue from use of materials or information contained in this work. The Haworth Press is committed to the dissemination of ideas and information according to the highest standards of intellectual freedom and the free exchange of ideas. Statements made and opinions expressed in this publication do not necessarily reflect the views of the Publisher, Directors, management, or staff of The Haworth Press, Inc., or an endorsement by them.

Cover design by Jennifer M. Gaska.

Library of Congress Cataloging-in-Publication Data

Hequembourg, Amy.
    Lesbian motherhood : stories of becoming / Amy Hequembourg.
       p. cm.
    Includes bibliographical references.
    ISBN: 978-1-56023-686-3 (hard : alk. paper)
    ISBN: 978-1-56023-687-0 (soft : alk. paper)
    1. Lesbian mothers. 2. Motherhood. I. Title.
HQ75.53.H47 2007
306.874'3086643—dc22

2006035686

CONTENTS

Acknowledgments

Many professional and personal factors came together in my life to make this book possible. During graduate school, my participation in the Foucault Reading Group at the University at Buffalo greatly influenced my sociological perspective and exposed me to Deleuze's and Guattari's work. My mentor, Dr. Jorge Arditi, provided invaluable support and friendship during my dissertation and beyond. Dr. Christopher Mele provided practical advice, clarity, and a sense of humor when I most needed it. The mothers who welcomed me into their homes and shared their intimate stories have forever shaped my politics and career goals—without their kindness and candor, this book would not have been possible. More recently, my mentors at the University at Buffalo's Research Institute on Addictions, Drs. R. Lorraine Collins and Kathleen Parks, provided moral support as I sought a publisher for this book. Most important, my two best friends—my husband and my mother—have always been there to celebrate the highs and help me recover from the lows. Finally, those we have lost along the way—my father, my grandmother, and my mother-in-law—are in my thoughts with each new milestone.

Lesbian Motherhood: Stories of Becoming
© 2007 by The Haworth Press, Inc. All rights reserved.
doi:10.1300/5922_a

ABOUT THE AUTHOR

Amy L. Hequembourg, PhD, is a research scientist at the University at Buffalo's Research Institute on Addictions in Buffalo, New York. She has incorporated her earlier interests in gay and lesbian issues with addictions research to examine gender and sexual identity differences in alcohol use and alcohol-related victimization. Pilot findings from focus groups and surveys informed a recent NIH grant application for a Mentored Career Development Award. Prior achievements include several teaching awards, the University at Buffalo's College of Arts and Sciences Dissertation Fellowship, and the NIH Loan Repayment Program. She presents her research findings regularly at sociology and addictions-related professional conferences, and her work has appeared in numerous peer-reviewed journals. Dr. Hequembourg is a committee member in the Society for the Study of Social Problems' Family Division and secretary of the Western New York Gay, Lesbian, Bisexual, and Transgender Anti-Domestic Violence Committee. She serves as an ad-hoc reviewer for the *Journal of Marriage & the Family* and *Violence & Victims*. Her current research includes investigating gender and sexual identity differences in patterns of substance use and interpersonal victimization, including childhood sexual abuse, adult sexual assault, and intimate partner violence.

Introduction

Lesbian and gay parenting has captured the attention of many Americans. Popular entertainers and celebrities, such as Ellen DeGeneris and Rosie O'Donnell, have proclaimed their families to the world and revealed intimate details of their quest for parenthood. Popular television shows, such as *20/20,* have aired compassionate stories about children living in gay- and lesbian-headed families. However, despite greater publicity about these families, conservatives continue to resist their inclusion in mainstream definitions of family. Tolerance has its limitations, as illustrated by Florida's steadfast resistance to the legalization of adoptions by lesbians and gays. In response, lesbian- and gay-headed families have more forcibly accentuated their similarities to other families, and academic studies validate their claims. Legal arguments center on the debate over similarity and difference, emphasizing the effects of lesbian and gay parenting on children's outcomes. The resulting debate is a hodgepodge of extreme claims at both ends of the spectrum, either vehemently discounting differences between lesbian-headed and heterosexual families, or centralizing differences as weaknesses.

When I first spoke with lesbian mothers in the mid-1990s, I was motivated to demonstrate the ordinariness of their experiences by centralizing their similarities to other mothers. However, in the midst of interviewing lesbian moms about their experiences, I realized that I was missing something. That "something" was unclear; however, it compelled me to reconsider the lens through which I was viewing lesbian parenting. One thing became apparent after talking with lesbian mothers: the vibrancy of lesbian parenting and the diversity of experiences among mothers are diminished by the larger cultural emphasis on their similarities to and differences from other mothers. Lesbian mothers *do* share many commonalities with heterosexual

Lesbian Motherhood: Stories of Becoming
© 2007 by The Haworth Press, Inc. All rights reserved.
doi:10.1300/5922_01

1

mothers, as indicated by a vast body of academic research. They parent in similar ways, and their children mature in similar ways to that of other children. However, that is only part of their stories. Floating beneath these similarities are complex lines and flows of practices that contradict and intersect those seamless stories of similarity. To understand the ways that these forces come together to create subjectivities, we must understand the discourses that attempt to stabilize stories of similarity. Hegemonic discourses on lesbian motherhood come from academic, legal, and popular spheres. In this book, I follow DiQuinzio's (1999, pp. 1-2) conceptualization of ideology and hegemony. "Ideology" refers to:

> . . . a discursive formation or a set of ideas deeply connected to and dependent on each other for their coherent articulation. Ideological formations attempt to systematize, rationalize, and justify particular material conditions and the social relations, structures, institutions, and practices to which these material conditions give rise. At the same time, ideological formations contribute to the production and maintenance of the material conditions and the social relations, structures, institutions, and practices that these formations claim simply to describe.

Ideological formations are also often hegemonic in nature. Thus, they are often perceived as "common sense" and taken-for-granted aspects of everyday life. Their commonsensical nature obscures the contradictions that are implicit in these formations and the practices that accompany them.

> To the extent that ideological formations prevent such contradictions from becoming evident and becoming a concern to a significant number of people, the vision of "the way things are" that these formations embody tends to be widely accepted and infrequently questioned. (DiQuinzio, 1999, p. 2)

Throughout this book, I introduce and revisit these various discursive formations of lesbian motherhood to illustrate the hegemonic forces that seek to stabilize subjects and conceal the workings of power that oppress and silence lesbian mothers.

One of my central goals in this book is to address a major concern among many feminists, post-structuralists, and queer theorists: how to better understand subjectivities that are discursive and constituted entirely by generative powers. Much has been written on this topic from a theoretical perspective (e.g., Butler, 1990, 1993; Foucault, 1990), but rarely is theory applied to the narrated experiences of everyday people. While the question of the post-structural subject and the notion of resistance within a generative power have long been of interest to me (Hequembourg & Arditi, 1999), I did not originally intend to make it the center of my analysis of lesbian motherhood. Instead, this path emerged as a result of the fractures and inconsistencies that emerged within the narratives of the lesbian mothers with whom I spoke.

Forty lesbian mothers volunteered to share with me their stories of parenting, family life, and coming-out during lengthy open-ended interviews conducted in the late 1990s. Similar to much of the research on lesbian motherhood, the women who participated in my study were mostly white, middle-class professionals. Undeniably, their social location shaped their philosophical and experiential approach to parenting as lesbian women. Furthermore, I spoke with them as a heterosexual woman with no children, which undoubtedly influenced the presentation of their stories to me, as well as my understanding and presentation of their narratives. We met in their homes, coffee shops, and restaurants for hours at a time, during which they spoke of their own experiences with very little guidance from me. Prior to the interview, the respondents were mailed a copy of a short autobiographic account of a lesbian mother's coming-out and family formation experiences. Their reactions to this story sometimes created an opening to begin the interview, while in other cases, the women's comfort level allowed them to immediately launch into stories about their personal experiences. Many of their stories centered on their similarity to heterosexual parents and the "normality" of their everyday lives as single mothers, partnered mothers, coparents, adoptive mothers, divorced mothers, and so on. I found their emphasis on similarity unsurprising, because it reflected much of what has been articulated in both academic studies about lesbian motherhood and autobiographical accounts written by lesbian mothers. However, as I listened more closely, subtle dislocations in their stories of similarity began to emerge. It was those disruptions and contradictions that became my primary interest.

My first encounters with the respondents' stories were influenced by the growing body of research about lesbian mothers. However, my attempts to understand their experiences within this framework left much to be desired, because it failed to account for the subtle inconsistencies and complexities within the mothers' narratives. My early attempts led to an understanding that fixed their narratives into inflexible categories of experience that followed the resistance/assimilationism approach commonly employed in the lesbian motherhood literature. In this literature, "assimilationism" refers to a constellation of discursive practices aimed at emphasizing similarity as a strategy to attain equality. Assimilationist strategies and tactics, although diverse, typically seek social change that will facilitate gay, lesbian, bisexual, and transgender (GLBT) integration into existing social structures. These strategies are similar to those employed by liberal feminists. An example would be legislation aimed at the legalization of same-sex marriages. Assimilationists advocate changes in marriage laws to allow "two people" to marry rather than "a man and a woman." The legalization of same-sex marriage through a change in the wording of existing laws would simply integrate same-sex couples into the existing marriage system, leaving it unaltered except for the gender of the spouses. Bruce Bawer (1993, p. 86) articulated this stance in his well-known book appropriately titled *A Place At the Table:*

> Gays exist as a group, then, largely because there is anti-gay prejudice. If gay relationships were taken for granted by everyone and accorded the same legal and moral status as heterosexual marriages, and if gay children were educated to be as comfortable with their sexuality as straight children and given courtship rituals comparable to those of straight children, much of what we think of as the "gay subculture" would disappear.

The contrasting approach to assimilationism, "resistance," has diverse and varying definitions within sociological literature. Resistance commonly

... implies the existence of a subject, at least partially autonomous, who actively opposes the structures of domination and who develops a sustained strategy of opposition. [. . .] It suggests at least partial autonomy from the structures of domination. It suggests the existence of a constituted subject who, nevertheless, can go beyond the field of power that generates the oppression and marginalization at the root of the resistance, and that constitutes him or her as subject to begin with. (Hequembourg & Arditi, 1999)[1]

In contrast to this use of the term "resistance," I will argue throughout this book that strategies of resistance involve more than a reaction or practice of appropriation in response to structures of domination. Following Foucault's logic, subjects can never step outside power and, consequently, "resistance" must be reconceptualized.

This oft-used assimilationism/resistance framework has had much utility for accounts of lesbian motherhood in prior research. However, I became discouraged in my early analysis, as it seemed to concretize the respondents into subject positions that reflected only a rigid and limited understanding of their narrated experiences. It was at that point that I was attracted to the work of Gilles Deleuze and Felix Guattari, who provide a complex understanding of the discursive nature of subjectivity. My reading of the respondents' narratives through Deleuze's and Guattari's theoretical lens forms the heart of this book. My perspective is also shaped by Judith Butler's and Michel Foucault's influential writings about the discursive nature of subjectivity and the workings of power that generate our understandings of self and subjectivities. My reading is only one among many that could be chosen; however, it is my hope that my account of the mothers' "becomings" captures the complexities of the respondents' narratives that would not be found in other analyses. Analyses of discursive formations focusing on the slippages, exclusions, and contradictions within these formations can lead to alternative readings that help dislodge "essentialistic" identity categories that are confining and exclusive to other articulations of experience (DiQuinzio, 1999, p. 2).

Throughout this book, I understand "discourses" as more than merely language. "A discourse is not a language or a text but a historically, socially, and institutionally specific structure of statements, terms, categories, and beliefs" (Scott, 1988, p. 35). Foucault formulates "discourses" as practices that are lived, acted out, and spoken by individuals. "Discourses, according to Foucault (1986), are comprised of statements which must be spoken from somewhere and by someone, and this speaking entails the *bringing into being* and positioning of a subject and assignment of a 'subject position' " (Harding 1998, p. 20, author's emphasis). Discourses are constituted by power and operate as fluid fields and mobile sets of relations. Discursive fields emerge through the (fleeting) historically situated coagulation of power relations.

> Neither the body nor thoughts and feelings have meaning outside their discursive articulation, but the ways in which discourse constitutes the minds and bodies of individuals is always part of a wider network of power relations, often with institutional bases. (Weedon, 1987, p. 108)

Foucault (1979) suggested that the elaboration of meaning involves conflict and power. He argued that meanings are locally contested within discursive "fields of force." Thus, the power to control a particular field resides in claims to (scientific) knowledge that are embodied in writing, as well as in disciplinary and professional organizations, institutions (hospitals, prisons, schools, factories, etc.), and social relationships (doctor/patient, teacher/student, employer/worker, parent/child, husband/wife, etc.). Discourse is thus contained or expressed in organizations and institutions as well as in words; all of these constitute texts or documents to be read (Scott, 1988).

Discursive fields are both enabling and constraining, as my analysis of the lesbian mothers' narratives in this book will demonstrate. "Discourses are *practices,* rather than structures or superstructures, that are lived, acted out and spoken by individuals" (Harding, 1998, p. 19). As practices, discourses generate and constitute subjectivities. In other words, subjects come into being and are positioned as a result of discursive practices (Harding, 1998). Thus, my focus in this book is not on stable, coherent lesbian mother subjects. Instead, I examine the ongoing, fluid, and multiple processes that generate subjects in discursive spaces. These "subjects" are what Deleuze and Guattari refer to as "becomings." Using their concepts, I weave a story of lesbian mothers' processes of "becoming," which slowly dismantles the categories that constitute the respondents and reveals the simultaneity of micro- and macropolitical movements that constitute subjectivities. Throughout this book, I take an analytical approach that emphasizes the mothers' interconnectedness to one another, to the structures that surround them, and their capacity to deploy lines of flight that escape those relations, while simultaneously being constituted by them. It is my conjecture that lesbian mothers pose an interesting case study to illustrate the ways that *all* subjectivities are borderless systems of flows and intensities. Essentially, we are all interconnected, and we exist in a perpetual state of "becoming." This approach challenges the ways that envision our "selves" and our political projects. It implies that we should begin to think of ourselves as bundles of flowing multiplicities rather than singular entities of Self.

In Chapter 1, I provide a critical overview of the academic and legal discourses associated with lesbian motherhood. My reading of this literature reveals a paradox: these discourses and their institutional practices merely expand the boundaries around acceptability rather than challenging them. In other words, these discourses and practices seek to include lesbian mothers within existing structures without fundamentally altering those structures. These limitations hinder our understanding of lesbian motherhood subjectivities and call for new ways of understanding the simultaneity of micro- and macropolitical movements.

Chapter 2 describes the forty lesbian mothers who shared their stories for this project, as well as details about the interview process.

In Chapter 3, I introduce Gilles Deleuze and Felix Guattari's analytical framework. They provide a dynamic way of understanding subjectivities that avoids dichotomous interpretations of social action (i.e., resistance or assimilationism) and focuses, instead, on the fluid and multiple lines of movement that constitute subjectivities. Movements consist of lines of flight that flee from the structured movement encouraged by hegemonic ideologies of lesbian motherhood, but also ultimately return to those structures so that both come to constitute subjectivities. The multiplicity of movements and flows that result are what Deleuze and Guattari characterize as "becomings."

Chapters 4 and 5 complement one another: Chapter 4 discusses some of the hegemonic ideologies surrounding motherhood in our culture, and Chapter 5 locates the forty mothers' life stories, alongside their understandings of motherhood. Deleuze and Guattari's analytical concepts are central to a discussion of the becoming processes of these respondents. I discuss the dilemmas faced and the strategies employed by respondents as they attempt to reconcile their sexuality with their mothering experiences. The central strategy to emerge is a normalization of parenting experiences. While these normalizing strategies clearly coincide with dominant interpretations of lesbian motherhood, they also reveal the inconsistencies and contradictions that fracture those stories. The respondents' stories about parenting decisions and struggles over infertility and conception further highlight these fractures.

The mothers' parenting stories were always foreshadowed by their stories about their sexual awakenings. In Chapter 6, I examine the respondents' stories about their sexual identities. They related stories about the nature of their lesbianism and others' reaction to the disclosure of their homosexuality. The women emphasize the genetic nature of their lesbianism and how little difference it makes in their everyday lives. However, woven throughout their stories is contradictory evidence of the intensities that make up micropolitical processes. The chapter finishes with stories about the mothers' perceptions of their children's sexual identities and how it relates to their lesbianism and personal coming-out experiences.

Throughout these chapters, I illustrate the respondents' propensity to depend on stories that emphasize normality and their similarity to other mothers (despite the fissures that are always present in their narrative accounts). However, some respondents clearly rejected those strategies of normalization. Chapter 7 provides an account of these women's stories and illustrates the diversity inherent in processes of "becoming." Tyler's and Michelle's stories reveal intensities of movements that embrace lines of flight rather than avoiding them. The book concludes with a discussion of the political implications of "becomings."

Chapter 1

Academic and Legal Depictions of Lesbian Motherhood: A Critique

Lesbian motherhood remained invisible in both mainstream society and much of the lesbian community prior to the 1970s (Shore, 1996; Arnup, 1995). Women were pressured to adhere to narrow ideologies of motherhood, and expressions of sexuality were discouraged, particularly when they involved nonheterosexual desire. Many lesbian mothers felt pressured to fragment their identities and maintain strict boundaries between their mothering activities and their sexualities. Lesbian separatists targeted the traditional notion of "family" as an oppressive institution that perpetuated heterosexism, thereby discouraging discussions of lesbian motherhood in their own communities (Shore, 1996; Stein, 1992).

The lesbian mothers who were most visible in the 1970s were those who gave birth to their children in the context of prior heterosexual relationships. A younger generation of lesbian women pursued new ways to become mothers, outside the bounds of a heterosexual relationship, as lesbianism slowly became more evident in mainstream culture. Sensibilities about motherhood slowly began to change and a wider array of mothering opportunities emerged for lesbians. Consequently, greater numbers of lesbian women chose to mother within the lesbian community. New reproductive technologies and greater availability of artificial insemination services contributed to growing numbers of lesbian women having children outside the bounds of heterosexual relationships.

Lesbian Motherhood: Stories of Becoming
© 2007 by The Haworth Press, Inc. All rights reserved.
doi:10.1300/5922_02

Conservative statistics indicate that there may be as many as five million lesbian women with children in the United States (Gottman, 1990; Rivera, 1979). Somewhere between one and nine million children are being raised by lesbian and gay parents.[2] According to Clunis and Green (1995, p. 11), "lesbian families are everywhere." These emerging alternative family forms are accompanied by a constellation of discourses aimed at understanding, analyzing, categorizing, comparing, regulating, and silencing lesbian-headed families. While some critics continue to vilify lesbian-headed families, a growing body of support, or at least tolerance for these families has slowly emerged in mainstream society. Discourses stressing tolerance have combined with lingering animosity toward lesbianism to become embedded in institutional structures that reflect and perpetuate a particular image of lesbian motherhood that underscores their "normality," and emphasizes the importance of their assimilation into dominant society. Lesbian mothers implicate themselves in these discourses as they constitute their subjectivities in ways that complement normalizing discourses about their parenting abilities. While some would characterize lesbian-headed families as assimilationists, due to their emphasis on normality, others argue that these families pose prospective sites for resistance to oppressive patriarchal family ideologies. These conflicting views make up an ongoing debate that revolves around assimilationism, resistance, similarity, and difference.

In this chapter, I provide a critical overview of the dominant academic approach to understanding lesbian motherhood. Academic discourses about lesbian motherhood emphasize the similarities between the parenting practices of lesbian women and other mothers. An understanding of these discourse helps explain how lesbian motherhood practices simultaneously strengthen dominant ideologies about motherhood and transform and subvert those ideologies. Academic interpretations of lesbian motherhood also influence legal interpretations of lesbian parenting. Through an overview of the legal climate surrounding lesbian motherhood and same-sex marriage, I show how academic discourses about lesbian motherhood are substantiated and validated in and through institutional structures. A careful reading of these discourses and institutional arrangements reveals a paradox, in which discourses and institutional practices merely expand the boundaries around acceptability rather than challenge them. Consequently, analyses focusing on the resistance/assimilationism or similarity/difference binary are limited in their capacity to grasp the complexity of lesbian motherhood subjectivities. These limitations are addressed, and the foundation is established for a discussion of my methodology in Chapter 2 and theoretical framework in Chapter 3.

RESISTANCE, ASSIMILATIONISM, OR BOTH?

A Critical Reading of Academic Discourses About Lesbian Motherhood

Do lesbian mothers challenge the very foundations of patriarchal ideologies that centralize biological ties and heterosexual unions as the basis for "family"? Or, are lesbian families just like other families? If so, why aren't lesbian mothers given equal access to parenting privileges? Is it best to seek equal rights by stressing similarities or by recognizing and validating their unique differences?

Most lesbian motherhood researchers write from a perspective that encourages assimilationism. Qualitative studies conducted by social workers, sociologists, and educators constitute the bulk of existing research about lesbian motherhood. Researchers often disclose their own lesbian mothering as a motivating factor for their research. Janet Wright (1998, p. 1) divulges her agenda in the opening pages of her book about lesbian stepfamilies:

> This book began over fifteen years ago out of pain—like many good ideas. My first experience in a lesbian step family, although it held the possibility (and even at times the actuality) of much good, was ultimately more painful than healthy. It was in the midst of this experience that I returned to school to get my PhD in social welfare. From the beginning, my concern about my own family's welfare, and my concern for the many lesbian step family members that I knew who were also in pain, fueled my desire to learn about and share information about lesbian step families. I could find no information on the topic, which only increased my desire to understand.

Wright also hoped to reveal strategies that promote successful parenting among lesbians: "My greatest hope is that this book will provide some of that knowledge and support for lesbian step family members, their allies, and their counselors" (Wright, 1998, p. 2). Many lesbian motherhood scholars share Wright's admirable agenda. Consequently, their research focuses on the similarities between lesbian mothers and other mothers and downplays the impact of sexuality on lesbian women's parenting abilities. Ellen Lewin (1993, p. 4), for example, admitted that she felt her "responsibility would be to demonstrate that lesbians were at least *ordinary* mothers, and therefore likely to be 'as good as' heterosexual mothers in comparable social and economic circumstances."

Emphasizing Similarities: Assimilationism As a Parenting Strategy

A prolific body of research emerged in the early 1980s to explore the psychological and social outcomes of children raised by lesbian mothers. The findings from these studies repeatedly underscored the similarities between children raised by lesbian mothers and heterosexual mothers (for reviews, see Victor & Fish, 1995; Patterson, 1995; Belcastro, Gramlich, Nicholson, Price, & Wilson, 1993; Parks, 1998). The demand from the legal sector for conclusive evidence about childhood outcomes spurred the emergence of this research.

Research indicates that children of lesbian mothers are not more likely to become homosexuals themselves (Golombok, Spencer, & Rutter, 1983; Gottman, 1990; Green, 1978; Tasker & Golombok, 1995), and they have similar mental health outcomes (Golombok, Spencer, & Rutter, 1983; Kirkpatrick, Smith, & Roy, 1981; Kirkpatrick, 1987). Empirical findings do not indicate that children of lesbian parents bear an unfair burden as a result of stigmatization (Green, Mandel, Hotvedt, Gray, & Smith, 1986; Patterson, 1994; Lott-Whitehead & Tully, 1993; Hare, 1994). Furthermore, studies indicate that lesbian mothers have parenting abilities and experiences similar to heterosexual mothers (Harris & Turner, 1986; Golombok, Spencer, & Rutter, 1983; Green et al., 1986; Hoeffer, 1981; Miller, Jacobsen, & Bigner, 1981).

This body of research provides powerful evidence to support legal and social equity claims by lesbian parents, despite methodological limitations (e.g., small sample sizes, overemphasis on cross-sectional studies, sample homogeneity, infrequent use of control groups, and sample bias; Gottman, 1990). The dominant theme to emerge in this literature is that lesbian mothers are more similar to heterosexual mothers than they are different from those mothers. Normality is glorified, and lesbian mothers' similarities to other mothers are espoused as the ideal goal for all lesbian-headed families. For example, the author of a popular gay and lesbian parenting manual (Martin, 1993, p. 6) proclaims, "I look forward to time when the designations 'parent' and 'lesbian' or 'gay man' are so completely, casually, and familiarly compatible that no one will ever have to deny a part of themselves again."

An approach predicated on similarity implies that parenting is a natural right that should not be denied to anyone based on their sexual orientation, because sexual orientation has little bearing on parenting abilities. Furthermore, strategies that emphasize the similarities between lesbian-headed families and heterosexual families imply that the heterosexual family is the ideal family form against which all variations of family should be measured. Research that holds preconceived expectations about the preponderance of similarities between lesbian mothers and heterosexual mothers advocates assimilationism into existing ideological systems of family as the ideal goal for all lesbian mothers. Unfortunately, this strategy marginalizes those who fail to conform to the ideal. Differences between lesbian-headed families and heterosexual families, and among lesbian parents, are silenced or ignored in an attempt to legitimate lesbian-headed families.

In a well-publicized article appearing in a leading sociological journal, Judith Stacey and Timothy Biblarz (2001) point out a paradox in the research on the parenting skills and outcomes of those children raised by lesbian mothers. They argue that well-intentioned sympathizers have inadvertently constructed an empirical image of lesbian-headed families that does injustice to their specificities. Through a careful analysis of existing research findings, Stacey and Biblarz conclude that family researchers consistently underscore lesbian-headed families' similarities with other families, while overlooking the small but interesting differences that arise in and through their day-to-day practices. They (2001, p. 179) argue that scholarly studies of lesbigay families provide an exciting opportunity to examine how sex and gender identities develop, the impact of family composition on childhood outcomes, and social implications for varied "biosocial routes to parenthood."

Strength in Diversity

Critics of a politics of normality argue that the differences in family life among lesbian-headed families should be embraced as a sign of strength rather than weakness. From this perspective, differences should be recognized as a result of homophobia rather than due to innate differences in parental skills and abilities based on sexual orientation. The goal of a "strength in diversity" strategy is to present lesbian-headed families as legitimate family structures that have been marginalized due to their differences rather than inadequacies. Consequently, lesbian mothers are valorized as pioneers who battle ignorance and prejudice in their attempts to forge a family. The lessons learned from these battles make lesbian parents stronger than those whose parenting rights are unquestioned. For example, Clunis and Green (1995), authors of *The Lesbian Parenting Book: A Guide to Creating Families and Raising Children,* acknowledge distinctions between lesbian-headed families and heterosexual parents, but also point out the distinctions *among* lesbian-headed families. They argue that this diversity is one of lesbian parents' greatest strengths:

> Good parenting is one of the greatest gifts you can give to the world, to your children and to yourself. As you take the lessons learned from surviving in a heterosexual world and empower your children to live differently, you give the gift of rising above bigotry and of celebrating diversity. As we move into the twenty-first century, the world will need women and men who know in their hearts and souls that difference is not to be feared, it is to be celebrated. (Clunis & Green, 1995, p. 7)

Lesbian Motherhood As a Means of Resistance to Patriarchy

Other politically motivated academic scholars endorse lesbian motherhood as a mechanism for overcoming heterosexual privilege and patriarchal oppression. Wald (1997, p. 181), for example, characterizes lesbian parents as a "culture of outlaw mothers" because they

> . . . threaten the traditional structure of the family as the male role is deleted and childrearing becomes the result of a purely

female choice. Including lesbian experiences expands the meaning of motherhood and challenges the assumption that a woman's biology predetermines her subordinate role in the traditional family and in society generally. Lesbian motherhood exposes the social creation of gender; it illustrates the possibilities of self-definition and of organizing alternative family structures that are removed from the traditional one-mother/one-father model. (Wald, 1997, p. 182)

From this perspective, lesbian motherhood is a radical strategy that challenges existing social structures and institutions in ways that are overlooked by those researchers who focus on assimilationism or diversity. It implies that lesbian mothers' everyday parenting insidiously subverts the power structures that support and validate patriarchy. Wald's (1997) approach takes the diversity approach in the previous section one step further to argue that lesbian motherhood potentially subverts and transforms traditional gender roles.

Using a similar rationale, Dunne (2000, p. 11) argues that the mundane ways that lesbian couples divide household and childcare responsibilities represent "a radical and radicalizing challenge to heterosexual norms that govern parenting roles and identities." Furthermore, lesbian parenting

. . . undermines traditional notions of the family and the heterosexual monopoly of reproduction. The same-sex context together with successful collaboration with donors supports the refashioning of kinship relationships. An attentiveness to the gender dynamics of sexuality illuminates further contestations. [. . .] (T)heir structural similarities as women place them in contradiction with dominant gender practices enacted in heterosexual relationships. This facilitates the evaluation and negotiation of more egalitarian approaches to work and parenting, and through their "operationalization," much of the logic supporting conventional divisions of labor is undermined. (Dunne, 2000, p. 11)

In other scholarly writings, lesbian motherhood is depicted as a challenge to the "very foundation upon which the notion of family has been based, namely heterosexuality" (Clunis & Green, 1995, p. 12). These proclamations are exciting, because they suggest that lesbian mothering strategies both intentionally and unintentionally challenge and subvert patriarchy.

In general, strategies of resistance aim to transgress the "heteronormative" boundaries that constitute and oppress gays and lesbians. The ideation of an autonomous subject that can transcend the boundaries imposed by structures of domination is implicit in these strategies. In simplistic terms, such strategies assume one can "free" himself or herself from structures of domination. Essentially, this assumes that lesbian mothers can step outside the roles offered by heteronormativity and forge new ones that transgress the boundaries constructed through relations of domination. However, a politics of transgression faces an inherent paradox in its assumptions about autonomy, because the agent is assumed to be autonomous from the very structures that define him or her (Hequembourg & Arditi, 1999).

Strategies of resistance are inextricably linked to the relations of domination in which they are deployed and, thus, may be powerless for instigating political change. Foucault is well-known for recognizing that "resistance is never in a position of exteriority in relation to power" (Foucault, 1990, p. 95). A resistance that is forever conceived internal to the power that generates it clearly complicates our conventional notions of subjectivity and the subject's ability to instigate changes to existing structures from a position external to that power. Power, according to Foucault, is not a possession belonging to a subject, but rather, a network of power *relations* that are constantly shifting and redistributing through the deployment of power mechanisms.

> [M]ore often one is dealing with mobile and transitory points of resistance, producing cleavages in a society that shift about, fracturing unities and effecting regroupings, furrowing across individuals themselves, cutting them up and remolding them, marking off irreducible regions in them, in their bodies and minds. (Foucault, 1990, p. 96)

Thus, power is not arranged hierarchically with subjects wielding power as a mechanism of control over others; rather, it manifests as a plurality of resistances. "Resistance" can no longer be conceived as a means to an end through the deployment of power. Instead, resistance is an ongoing play of generative, rather than restrictive, micropolitical forces. Mechanisms of power or strategic movements, consequently,

often have multiple effects that cannot be categorized in tidy definitions of transgression or assimilation (Hequembourg & Arditi, 1999).

These understandings of power and resistance have motivated
some lesbian motherhood researchers to suggest that lesbian parenting
strategies should be understood as combinations of resistance and
assimilationism.

Lesbian Motherhood As Resistance and Assimilationism

Ellen Lewin (1995, 1998) argues that lesbian mothers resist dominant structures of domination *and* reinforce oppressive structural institutions. In her research, she found that a notable difference between
lesbian mothers and heterosexual mothers is their route to pregnancy.
Lesbian women hoping to have children must not only work against
heteronormative definitions of motherhood, but also overcome mechanisms that resist their attempts to mother. Their successful challenge
of these oppressive mechanisms qualifies them as "resistors." However, according to Lewin (1998), lesbian mothers are not only "resistors" but also "accommodators," because they often emphasize their
motherhood over their lesbianism and subsequently reinforce traditional gender boundaries that separate mothers from nonmothers.
Lesbian mothers do not dramatically alter ideologies of womanhood;
rather, they expand that definition and reinforce the divisions between
women who mother and those lesbian and heterosexual women who
are not mothers. Lewin (1998, p. 335) concludes that lesbian mothers
should be thought of as "strategists" who use available cultural resources about motherhood to achieve their goals rather than merely
"resistors" or "accommodators."

> While such women are often conscious resisters, others gladly
> organize their experience as a reconciliation with what they
> view as traditional values. At the same time that some outsiders
> may see their behavior as transgressive (and thereby label them
> resisters or subversives), others perceive lesbian motherhood
> (along with other indications of compliance with conventional
> behaviors, such as gay/lesbian marriage) as evidence that lesbi-
> ans (and other "deviants") can be domesticated and tamed.

In Kath Weston's (1991) widely read study of gay and lesbian kinship systems, she makes similar conclusions about assimilationism.

> Rather than representing a crystallized variation of some mythically mainstream form of kinship, gay families simply present one element in a broader discourse on family whose meanings are continuously elaborated in everyday situations of conflict and risk, from holidays and custody disputes to disclosures of lesbian or gay identity. (Weston, 1991, pp. 199-200)

Dalton and Bielby (2000, p. 38) note that lesbian mothers "rely on gender as a resource for actively reconstructing the institution of the family." Therefore, lesbian mothers play a dual role in perpetuating current gender ideologies and forging new ones through their parenting practices. "Examining how their interactional strategies and practices are accomplished and understood yields insight into how lesbian mothers effect change in institutional definitions of the family *and* alter gendered conceptualizations of the two-parent family" (Dalton & Bielby, 2000, p. 38, my emphasis). This body of research clearly helps us to expand our understanding of how both structure and agency are intertwined in lesbian motherhood practices. However, it is limited, because it continues to operate within a theoretical framework based on a binary division between resistance and assimilation. Furthermore, this research does not usually account for the institutional structures in which discourses of lesbian motherhood have become realized.

In the following section, I expand on these academic discourses of lesbian motherhood to illustrate the ways in which these discourses are articulated in the legal system. Academic discourses are intertwined with these institutions and often work alongside them to dismantle negative images of lesbian parenting and contribute to the formation of an ideal for these families. Ellen Lewin (1993, p. xv), for example, acknowledged the need for research on lesbian motherhood because

> . . . there was an obvious need to generate knowledge about this highly stigmatized population, first, to make its existence visible, and second, to help dispel the stereotypes that prevailed in custody challenges and that could be considered responsible for injustices in the resolution of these cases.

Lewin's desire to overcome negative misconceptions about lesbian motherhood in order to advance their social standing, particularly in the legal system, is a common theme among lesbian motherhood legal scholars. Prominent researchers (Polikoff, 1982, 1990, 1991) are widely cited in legal cases involving lesbian-headed families. The following section is not intended as an exhaustive overview of the legal advances made by lesbian mothers nor is it intended to justify legal strategies aimed at assimilationism. Instead, I provide a brief overview of legal discourses about lesbian motherhood in order to illustrate how various ideologies about lesbian motherhood have become interconnected and realized within social institutions.

LEGAL STRUCTURES: THE SEDIMENTATION OF ACADEMIC DISCOURSES INTO INSTITUTIONAL STRUCTURES

Historically, lesbian mothers have struggled for legal recognition of their families and their right to parent. Lesbian mothers first caught the attention of the courts in the 1980s when they were embroiled in custody battles with their exhusbands (i.e., the biological father of their children). An entire body of legal discourses emerged to address the complexities of these cases. Until the early 1990s, these cases dominated public consciousness about lesbian motherhood. Only recently has the legal system begun addressing the vista of emerging lesbian motherhood experiences, such as those involving lesbian couples who conceive together as a couple using artificial inseminations. In this section, I chose a few interesting illustrations of the various ways that lesbian mothers have entered the court system, the resulting legal discourses that have emerged in response to these varying family forms, and the implications of these discourses for the ways that we conceive of lesbian mothers and the ways that they conceive of themselves.

Custody Disputes

The United States court system has resisted adapting its definitions of family to accommodate lesbian-headed families. For many decades, lesbian mothers feared the loss of custody of their children due to their lesbianism. Most lesbian mothers gave birth during a prior heterosexual marriage until the "gayby" boom in the last decade. Courts relied on outdated medical definitions of lesbianism as a form of psychological deviancy during much of the 1980s. Therefore, lesbianism often became the sole criteria by which parenting abilities were assessed by the courts. Court decisions relied on the "per se rule," which divests trial courts of the power to grant custody to particular individuals, simply because they fall within certain categories that are classified as unfit or undesirable. Petitioning gay or lesbian individuals were regularly categorized as unfit and automatically disqualified as potential parents under the "per se rule." The per se rule assumes that interests of the child will never be furthered by having gay or lesbian parents (Starr, 1998). Unfortunately, some state legal systems still favor this approach, although greater numbers of courts across the nation are replacing the "per se rule" with the nexus approach. In a notable Virginia case in the early 1990s, Sharon Bottoms lost parental custody to her mother based on a conservative interpretation of a 1986 Virginia Supreme Court decision finding gay and lesbian parents automatically unfit to parent. Fortunately, the Bottoms case was not universally representative of all states in the United States in the 1990s, but there continue to be similar conservative interpretations of older laws concerning the parental rights of gays and lesbians. Florida laws, for example, explicitly outlaw adoptions by gay and lesbian individuals, and Mississippi and Utah prohibit gay and lesbian couples from adopting children.[1]

Meanwhile, progressive state court decisions are beginning to recognize the viability of lesbian-headed families (Starr, 1998; Maxwell, Mattijssen, & Smith, 2000). Studies about the positive outcomes of children raised by lesbians are often employed as defense strategies in successful court cases. This research is useful in defense of lesbian parental rights, because it reveals few differences between children raised in heterosexual households and those raised by lesbian mothers. These findings have been one of the major tools that lawyers employ to defend the interests of lesbian women involved in custody disputes with their former husbands (i.e., the biological father of their children). Cases involving second-parent adoptions also rely on these findings as a means of legitimating nonbiological mothers' parenting roles. For example, in one of the earliest successful second-parent adoption case in New York State (i.e., *In the Matter of Evan*), eleven studies were cited to illustrate that there were no significant differences between children raised by heterosexual parents and those raised by gay and lesbian parents.

There has been a gradual decrease in court cases involving blatant discrimination against lesbian parents based solely on sexual orientation. However, change is slow due to the legal process by which decisions occur in lower courts and only move to higher courts upon appeal. Laws about gay and lesbian parental rights often differ substantially from state-to-state and even county-to-county within the same state. Unfortunately, there are still many conservative locales where judges continue to discriminate against gay and lesbian parents based on their sexual orientation.

To overcome the potential for blatant discrimination based on sexual orientation, many courts employ a "nexus approach" in deciding these cases.

> The nexus standard requires that there be a clear connection (or "nexus") between a parent's sexual identity and harm to the child before the parent's sexual orientation assumes any relevance in a custody, visitation, or adoption dispute. Under this approach, the sexual orientation of a parent alone cannot form the basis of denying parenting rights unless it is demonstrated to cause harm to the child.[2]

Regrettably, the nexus approach is not foolproof, and unsympathetic judges can find other ways to deny access to rights and privileges to lesbian-headed families. *The Lesbian and Gay Parents' Legal Guide to Child Custody* (1989, p. 10) warns lesbian and gay parents that

> In most states, a judge cannot decide that you are unfit simply because you are lesbian or gay. However, you do not have to be unfit to be denied custody. A judge can determine that it is not in the best interest of the child for you to have custody even if you are a perfectly fit parent. A judge may also weigh other factors more heavily against you in assessing best interest because you are lesbian or gay, without openly saying that sexual orientation is the reason for denying custody.

Second-Parent Adoption and Custody Disputes Between Lesbian Comothers

Courts also are faced with an increasingly complex array of lesbian family formation issues. Early court cases primarily involved lesbian women who were fighting exhusbands for custody of their children. Contemporary courts are forced to consider the implications of biology on family relationships as more women are having children together as a couple using alternative inseminations (AI). Until recently, family courts relied almost universally on the biological connection between a child and petitioning parties in order to make their custody decisions. However, as more cases involving AI couples reached the attention of the courts, narrow legal definitions of "parent" have come under scrutiny. Because many states do not allow same-sex marriage, lesbian couples must seek other legal means to protect their parenting rights.

Second-parent adoptions have become a popular avenue for nonbiological mothers to protect their parental rights. Second-parent adoption differs from traditional adoption in that it allows the biological mother to retain legal custody while creating a second, legally recognized parental status for the second mother.[3] However, not all states and counties currently recognize nonbiological lesbian mothers' rights to seek second-parent adoption, and it is only a legally viable option for *some* lesbian mothers.[4]

Nonbiological mothers whose partners gave birth using an unknown donor most commonly pursue second-parent adoption. In contrast, biological mothers whose children have a legally recognized parental relationship with their biological father must first convince the father to rescind his parental rights before their partner can seek second-parent adoption. This is a stumbling block for many blended families. Those mothers who, for whatever reason, are unable to contact the biological father of their child also are unable to pursue second-parent adoption.[5]

Other factors also affect women's decisions to seek second-parent adoption. The economic costs of hiring a lawyer are too high for some mothers. Some lesbian couples do not pursue second-parent adoption because they find the required home visits too intrusive.

Those who have a history of drug abuse or incarceration also are prevented from adopting. Ignorance about lesbian and gay family rights among lawyers is common, leaving many lesbians unaware that second-parent adoption rights exist. Many nonbiological mothers do not have legally recognized parental relationships with their children as a result of these factors. This can become a point of contention when a couple separates and litigation for custody ensues.

When custody disputes between biological mothers and lesbian comothers first appeared, "parental rights" were narrowly interpreted resulting in loss of custody by most petitioning comothers. Until the early 1990s, second-parent adoptions did not exist and, consequently, nonbiological coparents were unable to secure legal parental rights under any circumstances. Thus, nonbiological coparents were at the mercy of their ex-partners (i.e., biological mothers) when they separated. Recently, however, there has been a legal trend toward emphasizing "psychological parenting" or "social parenting" in the consideration of these cases. This concept first appeared in heterosexual custody disputes

> . . . as a means of shifting the focus of custody disputes away from the rights of the biological parents to the best interests of the child, as manifested by the child's need for stability and continuity with regard to relationships with significant others in the child's life. The psychological parent may be a biological parent but is not necessarily so. Rather, the psychological parent is the individual who has fulfilled the child's "psychological needs for a parent." (Goldstein, Freud, & Solnit, 1973, p. 98)

For example, a New Jersey custody case involving a separated lesbian couple was ultimately decided on the merit of "psychological parenting."[6] V.C. and M.J.B. had been together for six years, during which time they had twins together via artificial insemination. When they separated, the biological mother (M.J.B.) allowed her partner (V.C.) to have visitation with their children for several months, after which she rescinded those rights. With no legal or biological ties to her children, V.C. sued for legal recognition as a parent. The New Jersey lower court initially denied her plea for joint custody or visitation. Upon appeal, the decision was reversed in part, and V.C. was awarded visitation rights. M.J.B. further appealed the case to the Supreme Court of New Jersey where, in a surprising outcome, the judge upheld the decision and V.C. was granted visitation with the couple's twins. Many hailed this decision as an important victory for all non-biological lesbian coparents. However, the Supreme Court's decision merely upheld the lower court's earlier decision in New Jersey and did not alter the legislation in other states.

When this was written, there were only a few states (e.g., Wisconsin and Rhode Island) with similar legal frameworks for "psychological parenthood." Outdated laws are increasingly challenged for their narrow interpretation of "family" as more of these cases reach the courts in various states. However, these cases are revealing because they expose the assumptions underlying family law in the United States and illustrate the ways that academic discourses have become concretized in legal institutions and policies. I will return to more examples to illustrate this process later in this chapter, but, first, I want to explore the connection between legal and academic discourses about lesbian parenting.

Assimilation or Resistance? Implications of Legal Disputes Involving Lesbian Mothers

Legal cases reflect a certain institutionalization of the academic debates discussed earlier in this chapter. On the one hand, some legal theorists argue that legal definitions of "parent" and "family" need to be expanded to include lesbian-headed families. They argue that lesbian-headed families are similar to other families except that they include two mothers with differing biological relations with their children. This legal strategy assumes that the expansion of legal family definitions to include lesbian and gay families would result in lesbian-headed families becoming increasingly similar to other families, because they would have access to the rights and responsibilities associated with legally recognized family units.

Other legal theorists present a different strategy that contrasts with attempts to assimilate lesbian-headed families into existing legal theory. They argue that the current system is flawed and, consequently, few changes would result from the inclusion of lesbian-headed families. These legal theorists argue that the expansion of rights to include gays and lesbians would merely expand existing practices and discourses to include gays and lesbians without altering the law in any fundamental ways, thus further marginalizing those who don't conform to the new standard. These critics propose alternative ways of extending rights to lesbian-headed families. In the following sections, I explore this debate and propose the implications.

Legal Strategies in Favor of Assimilationism

Many gays and lesbians endorse a legal strategy aimed at expanding existing laws to include the needs of lesbian- and gay-headed families. This argument is a practical response to the concerns that U.S. lesbian and gay couples have about their limited legal parental rights.

Arlene Istar Lev (1998) wrote in a popular lesbian and gay parenting magazine about her experiences as a lesbian mother in order to accentuate the similarities and differences between lesbian-headed families and heterosexual-headed families. She pointed out that institutional validation is lacking for lesbian couples, thus forcing them to take other elaborate legal measures to protect their families. "My partner now carries power of attorney papers in her pocket at all times that clearly state her legal right to make medical decisions for our son should the need ever arise." She also explained that her will outlines her wish to give legal custody of their son to her partner in the event of her death. "In a heterosexual family, a medical doctor would automatically assume both parents rights to make medical decisions. A heterosexual parents' right to custody of her child in the event of the death of a spouse would not even come under the scrutiny of a court system."[7]

Like many other gays and lesbians, Istar Lev (1998) demands legal recognition of her family so they can access the legal rights afforded to other family relationships in the United States. According to The Lambda Legal Defense and Education Fund, there are a substantial number of legal and economic protections attached to legal marriage. These include sharing government benefits (e.g., social security and Medicare); filing joint tax returns to get special marriage or family rates or exemptions; having joint parenting, adoption, foster care, custody, and visitation; obtaining joint insurance policies for home and auto, as well as family health coverage; automatic inheritance in the absence of a will; securing equitable division of property and determine child custody and support in case of divorce; obtaining veterans' discounts on medical care, education, and housing loans; entering jointly into rental leases with automatic renewal of rights; making medical decisions on a partner's behalf in the event of illness; choosing a final resting place for a deceased partner; accessing bereavement or sick leave to care for partner or child; receiving spousal exemptions to property tax; obtaining wrongful death benefits for surviving partner and children; applying for immigration and residency for partners from other countries; obtaining domestic violence protection orders; and visiting a partner or child in the hospital and other public institutions. Most lesbian and gay couples and families do not automatically receive these benefits, because they are not able to legally marry. Lesbian and gay couples are denied access to benefits because most familial benefits are based on the assumption of heterosexuality and legal marriage. Consequently, the desire for the legalization of same-sex marriage is intertwined with lesbian and gay familial concerns. For many lesbian and gay parents, the prospect of legal marriage offers hope for legalizing their parental relationships to their children. According to Duclos (1991), same-sex marriage is important to lesbian and gay parents because it would legally legitimize their parental claims during custody disputes with heterosexual individuals or couples, former lesbian partners with genetic ties to their children, or in cases where the state argues that the children are in need of protection based on standardized tests. Legalized same-sex marriages, therefore, would potentially discourage judges from viewing gay and lesbian parents as a threat to the best interests of their children.

Vermont became the first state in the United States to legalize same-sex civil unions.[8] The court's ruling states,

> We hold that the State is constitutionally required to extend to same-sex couples the common benefits and protections that flow from marriage under Vermont law. Whether this ultimately takes the form of inclusion within the marriage laws themselves

or a parallel "domestic partnership" system or some equivalent statutory alternative, rests with the Legislature.

Mary Bernstein (2001, p. 436) points out that the inherent bias in Vermont's Supreme Court decision to grant civil unions to gay and lesbian couples is "Reminiscent of the notorious 'separate but equal' doctrine that mandated segregation for African Americans, the Vermont legislature discursively marked lesbian and gay unions as less than heterosexual marriages." Furthermore,

> Vermont's creation of civil unions provides a way to avoid the challenge to heteronormativity posed by same-sex marriage. By segregating lesbian and gay "marriages" under the rubric of "civil unions," heterosexual marriage remains the cultural norm distinct (and safe) from lesbian and gay civil unions. (Ibid., p. 439)

Massachusetts is currently the only state in the United States to allow legal same-sex marriage (in contrast to civil unions in states like Vermont and Connecticut). Attempts in other states, most notably in Hawaii, have met with open hostility and opposition by many legal institutions in the United States. President Clinton instituted the Defense of Marriage Act (DOMA) in response to the legal battle over same-sex marriage in Hawaii. Enacted in 1996 by the U.S. Congress, DOMA allows Congress to restrict legal definitions of "marriage" to unions between men and women and assures that states could not be required to recognize same-sex marriages legalized in other states (Culhane, 1999). Attempts to halt a nationwide legalization of same-sex marriage laws indicate the pervasiveness of homophobia and heteronormativity in the United States today.

Heteronormativity is defined as "the view that institutionalized heterosexuality constitutes the standard for legitimate and expected social and sexual relations" (Ingraham, 1999, p. 17). Heteronormativity consists of a wide range of discourses and practices that underlay heterosexual imagery and ensures that heterosexuality is revered as the model or ideal against which all other relationships are measured. By extension, it dictates what is "normal" and "abnormal" (Ingraham, 1999, p. 17). The consequences of heteronormativity are not benign for they make possible the grounds upon which various ideologies about marriage are constructed as well as determining the mechanisms for allocating benefits and responsibilities.

DOMA, and similar legal strategies, represent conservative efforts to maintain heteronormativity. Advocates for legalized same-sex marriage recognize the importance of this strategy for obtaining benefits and altering ideologies about gays and lesbians. These activists argue that positive pro-marriage rhetoric and the potential legalization of same-sex marriage would result in significant transformations in the ideologies associated with lesbian- and gay-headed families, thereby making same-sex relationships worthy of the same respect and benefits afforded heterosexual couples (Duclos, 1991). Pro-legalization strategies benefit the gay and lesbian community in general, because they emphasize the "... reality that many lesbians and gay men are involved in long term, intimate, caring relationship that are virtually indistinguishable from those entered into by heterosexuals" (Dalton, 1991, p. 4). The emphasis on normality and similarity in pro-marriage legalization strategies undermine negative ideologies that portray gays and lesbians as deviant and oversexed (Dalton, 1991).

In addition to merely altering ideologies about lesbian- and gay-headed families, the legalization of same-sex marriage might revolutionize the institution of marriage and radically alter societal views about sex and sexuality (Duclos, 1991). According to this perspective, married gay and lesbian couples would be the catalysts for radical social changes, potentially transforming the institution of marriage by subverting deeply ingrained notions of gender that reproduce unequal power relations between men and women.

Criticizing Assimilationism and Proposing Alternative Strategies of Resistance

Strategies aimed at the legalization of same-sex marriage and the inclusion of lesbian and gay parents into the existing legal rhetoric about "the family" are sometimes criticized as too assimilationist. Advocates of more radical strategies argue that the entire legal approach should be overhauled to include diversity rather than simply expanding the boundaries around acceptability. For example, one alternative is to broaden the definition of parenthood and permit "all those who fall within that definition to compete for custody using a best interests of the child standard, while preferring those who are within the definition to those who are not" (Polikoff, 1990, p. 473). This approach favors legal recognition of the diversity inherent in the term "family" and provides freedom to determine individual family needs based on differences in race, class, ethnicity, gender, and so on. However, this strategy risks marginalizing those who fail to conform to a standard built around existing institutionalized forms of family that assume the superiority of the nuclear, monogamous marital unit (Duclos, 1991).

Critics argue that assimilationist approaches to legalizing same-sex marriage ignore the historically damaging nature of the marital institution, because the centrality of marriage is never doubted or questioned (Duclos, 1991). Furthermore, these strategies may simply widen margins around acceptability and further marginalize those who fail to conform to the new standard of acceptability. Those who fail to conform to dominant expectations about "couplehood" could suffer increased isolation and discrimination, including denial of basic rights to which others are entitled (Bernstein, 2001). For example, those who value nonmonogamous relationships, those who have more than one permanent partner, those with open relationships, or those who simply do not want to get legally married would not conform to this standard and might be subsequently marginalized if same-sex marriage were legalized. Legal discourses of marriage are symbolically important for they reflect cultural values and have very real effects on daily family life. It also is possible that legally married gays and lesbians would join heterosexuals in condemning those who don't want to marry:

> After all, absent in-group consciousness raising, those who eschew vanilla couplehood will risk marginalization not only by straight society but also by lesbians and gay men who view them as a threat to their newfound "respectability." (Dalton, 1991, p. 5)

Similarly, Dennis Poplin (1997, p. 7) fears that diversity and difference are sacrificed when politics of normality are invoked: "When the circle is drawn around normal gays, who is left outside? If Ellen [DeGeneres] is normal then what is RuPaul?"

As an alternative to the "adding on" approach, Duclos advocates legislative changes that are no longer predicated on an ideal family type (i.e., heterosexual, nuclear family). These ideals, according to Duclos, are reflections of male power that preserve and enhance the privileges and powers associated with patriarchal institutions. The subtle workings of patriarchy maintain a facade of neutrality about gender in order to disguise the inequities inherent in societal institutions. Politics aimed at the legalizing of same-sex marriage merely reinforce heterosexist institutions, thus insidiously perpetuating the oppression of gays and lesbians. The debate over same-sex marriage is based on a host of dangerous assumptions:

> The hidden subject of this sentence is the state; it gets to give or withhold permission. Lesbians and gay men get lumped together into "homosexuals," an abstract and oversimplified sexualized label. Marriage is reified; it assumes a shape fixed by ideological and legal norms that "homosexuals" may or may not fit; the complexity and dynamism of this longstanding legal relationship is collapsed into the point of entry (marrying). The question is posed from the dominant perspective; the yes/no answer it commands presupposes a singularity (or essence) in the categories "homosexual" and "marriage" that does not actually exist. (Duclos, 1991, p. 31)

A legal approach that recognizes and validates diversity is necessary for overcoming these problems. Rather than imposing a universal ideal of family as a guidepost, Duclos (1991) argues that gay and lesbian activists should not depend on the legalization of same-sex marriage to bring about social change. Instead, activists should concentrate on instigating small changes that cumulatively lead to larger changes that affect the daily lives of gays and lesbians. A series of smaller changes would provide gays and lesbians the opportunity to actively choose the aspects of marriage that they find most beneficial and appealing, without forcing rigid institutionalization into their lives (Duclos, 1991).

Others have offered similar warnings about the dangers associated with attempts to achieve cultural transformations via legal changes. Bernstein (2001) argues that legal changes can and will be achieved if activists continue to centralize legal strategies that de-emphasize non-normative behaviors in gays' and lesbians' lives. These legal changes will inevitably better the daily material conditions faced by lesbians and gays and their families, but will accomplish little in terms of altering the stigmatized status of homosexuality (Bernstein, 2001).

Legal Inadequacies and Lesbian Custody Disputes

United States child custody cases involving lesbian parents reveal some of the weaknesses and pitfalls in assimilationist strategies. Many successful legal cases involving lesbian parents insidiously reflect a bias against lesbian-headed families even though they appear to be legal victories. This bias results from the consistent use of a family ideal against which lesbian couples are measured. Courts continue to measure lesbian mothers against this yardstick of parental viability although such an ideal is merely a legal construction that neglects the reality of most contemporary heterosexual and nonheterosexual families.

Successful second-parent petitions are particularly insightful in illustrating the terms of the discourses used by judges to rationalize their decisions to grant adoption rights to both parents. In these decisions, several factors are often cited as signs of a "healthy, functioning" family, including monogamy, duration of the relationship, economic security, commitment to the relationship, and sharing of parental responsibilities. For example, in the New Jersey Supreme Court's decision to uphold a lower court's decision to grant a nonbiological coparent's visitation rights they relied on a typology of the "ideal" mother and family as a central element in the assessment of the couple in question:

> Together, they went to see a fertility specialist and, after M.J.B. got pregnant, they jointly attended prenatal and Lamaze classes. V.C. [the petitioning nonbiological coparent] was in the delivery room when the twins—a boy and a girl—were born in September 1994. V.C. helped raise them, both emotionally and

financially, according to [the judge's] opinion. In 1995, V.C. and M.J.B. jointly purchased a home in Maplewood and went through a nonbonding "marriage" ceremony in which they declared their commitment as a family.

Similarly, *In the Matter of Caitlin and Emily,*[10] the court requested a home-study whose results were cited at length in the decision to allow their nonbiological mother second-parent adoption rights. I quote at length from this decision, because it is representative of the factors typically considered in second-parent adoption cases.

> . . . petitioning adoptive mother (M.E.F.), age 40, was graduated from the University of Notre Dame in 1975, with a Bachelor of Science degree in Biology. In 1976, she earned a Master's Degree in Engineering, with a concentration in Environmental Health. She is currently employed as an Environmental Engineer and provides the primary financial support to the family. Biological mother (P.B.), age 41, is not employed. M.E.F. and P.B. have known each other for 15 years and have lived together for 9 years. All of their possessions are joint ownership and each has a warm relationship with her nuclear family, visiting them often. The family lives in a larger two-story 100-year-old house in excellent repair, in a quiet neighborhood on a tree-lined street populated with young families. The home study concludes: P.B. and M.E.F. are two intelligent, stable, mature women who have been thoughtful and who have carefully considered their relationship and how they can be the best kind of parents for the two children. Both are excellent parents, with fine values, spiritually, culturally, educationally and emotionally. M.E.F. is a practicing Catholic and she has been highly recommended by her pastor. Both women understand that there will be questions they will have to deal with when their children become knowledgeable about the family lifestyle. It is my belief that they will deal with these concerns in a loving and honest manner. M.E.F.'s wish to adopt the children and parent them along with P.B. is a courageous and well thought through desire and I feel she will add much security and love to the children's lives. I strongly recommend this adoption. (B-F Homestudy, p. 7)

M.E.F. was assessed as a worthy parent based on her intelligence, education, professional status, adjustment, religiosity, and ability to help her children cope with potential bigotry due to their family composition.

As M.E.F.'s case illustrates, the ideal family constructed in these legal discourses is a middle-class, professional, two-parent home, with one parent preferably staying home with the children. This outdated expectation fails to account for the changing demographics of today's families. Furthermore, it is questionable whether or not these qualifications are the standard that we should ultimately be seeking. To do so, as I have already pointed out, marginalizes those who fail to conform to that standard. It also constructs an image of "normality" against which all individuals and families are measured. This has very real effects on people's daily lives. Foucault observed a similar phenomenon in the criminal justice system:

> . . . the sentence that condemns or acquits is not simply a judgment of guilt, a legal decision that lays down punishment; it bears within it an assessment of normality and a technical prescription for a possible normalization. Today, the judge—magistrate or juror—certainly does more than "judge." (Foucault, 1979, pp. 20-21)

Just as judges provide an unspoken "prescription for normalization" in criminal cases, they also determine which men and women are suitable for legal parental rights. The normalization that occurs in the discourses and practices of the courtroom are part of a larger system of interlocking mechanisms of power that trickle down to the level of everyday practices.

In Boyd's (1998) analysis of Canadian child custody decisions involving disputes between lesbian women and exhusbands (i.e., the biological father of their children), she argued that the nexus approach holds potentially dangerous implications for the way that lesbian mothers must present themselves in order to successfully retain custody of their children. According to Boyd (1998, p. 140), legal success is most often achieved among lesbian mothers who attempt to:

> . . . lead quiet, discreet (i.e., closeted) lives; to appear to the outside world to be heterosexual single parents; who indicate that

they will be more than happy if their children turn out to be heterosexual.

The emphasis in most of these court cases is to demonstrate lesbian or gay parents' ability to shield their children from a gay lifestyle, protect them from societal homophobia, and assure "normal" developmental outcomes for their children.

> This argument adopts and reinforces the thinly veiled fear of lesbians and gay men in society; that they are predatory, dirty, flagrant, etc. In turn, this approach creates a situation where a lesbian mother's ability to argue successfully for custody depends on her ability to convince judges that she lives on the safe side of the line between "good" and "bad" lesbians. (Boyd, 1998, p. 143)

Expert testimony on the "normal psychological development" of gay and lesbian parents (and their children) is often a central focus in child custody cases. The differences among heterosexual parents and lesbian parents are often obscured as a result of the interpretations made by legal experts based on academic evidence. Furthermore, lesbian parents are held accountable for reducing the stigma experienced by their children. In cases employing the nexus approach, lesbian parents must conform to the heterosexist ideal family form in order to prove their parental worth. As Boyd (1998) points out, biases emerge against those lesbian parents who depart from the heterosexual norm, which is the "measuring stick" against which all parental fitness is assessed.[11]

Julie Shapiro (1999) refers to the refinement of lesbian identities into heternormative definitions of normality as the "domestication" of lesbians. She argues that the second-parent adoption process forces lesbian women to mold themselves into a "good lesbian" model. Worthy lesbian mothers must "walk, talk, and act like heterosexual parents, and must conform to the nuclear family model" (Shapiro, 1999, p. 35). Fulfillment of the "good lesbian" model requires "cooperation, accommodation, and assimilation" (Ibid.). Furthermore, lesbian mothers must believe that "real" mothers are only those with legal parental rights. The constraining aspects of second-parent adoption laws are obscured by this domestication process.

Others agree that the current system unsuccessfully determines the needs of lesbian- and gay-headed families based on a family law system that is "resolutely heterosexual in its structure and presumptions" (Ettelbrick, 1993, p. 514). The current system presumes marital and biological connections as the basis of "family." Paula Ettelbrick (1993), an academic and lawyer who defends lesbian and gay parents, argues that the present system fails to account for the fact that "the very basic experiences of lesbians with regard to parenting are different from those of men and heterosexual women" (Ettelbrick, 1993, p. 515). Ettelbrick (1993) argues that courts should handle lesbian parent custody cases in ways that take into account the specificities of their differences rather than forcing them to conform to a preconceived ideal. Solutions and legal guidelines are needed that reflect the experiences of gay and lesbian parents, rather than forcing them "into the already confusing matrix of heterosexual family rights" (Ettelbrick, 1993, p. 553). Despite the wisdom of this advice, it fails to account for the multitude of ways that lesbian parents themselves embrace existing heterosexually-based legal discourses and make them their own.

This is often exemplified in custody disputes between separated lesbian parents who gave birth together using alternative insemination. The courts are seeing an increasing number of custody disputes in which a biological mother denies custody rights to her ex-partner, who did not have legal parenting rights, but served as a psychological parent to their children. During the ensuing custody battle, biological mothers often employ a legal strategy that centralizes her biological ties to her children while refuting her ex-partner's contribution to the parenting of their children. Consequently, the biological mother's defense strategy undermines the arguments commonly employed to seek the right to second-parent legal rights for lesbian women (like those described above).

For example, in a case involving a nonbiological mother fighting for joint custody of her ex-partner's biological children, the biological mother vehemently objected to the court's decision to allow the coparent custody rights. The biological mother employed language that reinforced the traditional biological basis of "family": "I will fight this all the way. She is not the parent. I'm the parent. It's cut and dried."[12] Furthermore, her lawyer substantiated these claims in her defense by arguing that the petitioning coparent was "a non-biologi-cal, non-adoptive, third-party stranger in the eyes of the court." Ac-cording to her lawyer, visitation rights against the wishes of the bio-logical mother (Christine) would be "an unconstitutional violation of Christine's due process rights."[13] The tactics taken by Christine and her lawyer included appearing in front of news cameras with her chil-dren in order "to let the public and all the parents know what this case involves . . . the legal rights of natural parents." Furthermore, she adds, "All of you natural parents out there: you have legal custody over your children, and nobody, not the court, not the state, can come in and take your children away. This is a small step, but a big step for the government to get its foot in the door."[14]

A nonbiological mother's success, in these cases, often depends on her defense of the superiority of her biological ties to her children, while undermining the nonbiological ties between her ex-partner and their children. The dangers of this approach have not escaped com-mentary by others who are concerned about the increasing visibility of these lesbian custody cases in our legal system. Gay & Lesbian Advocates & Defenders in Boston published an online guide de-signed to protect the standards for child custody in same-sex relation-ships in which they encourage gay and lesbian couples to plan ahead to avoid disputes that require legal intervention.[15] In a section entitled "Preventing Harm to Our Collective Interests," the authors warn that these custody cases use dangerous strategies, because they essen-tially invalidate the same arguments that are used to support second-parent adoption rights and other family benefits for gay and lesbian parents.

> We convey to the courts a disrespect for our own families when members of our own community insist that our relationships—of whatever duration and however intermingled—do not amount to a "family," or that the other parent was really nothing more than a babysitter.

They warn that these legal strategies can "undercut" attempts to se-cure legal rights for lesbian and gay parents and may "come back to haunt our community in many contexts." This warning serves to re-mind gay and lesbian couples that their daily practices have larger implications for discourses about family life and private life, in general. Even when a judge looks favorably on a lesbian woman's or couple's petition for custody rights, his or her decision is located in a context of dominant ideologies about family life that marginalize those who do not conform to this mold. For example, although the court case described earlier in this chapter involving V.C. and M.J.B. resulted in a nonbiological coparent gaining access to her children, V.C.'s victory was limited. Her original petition for shared custody was eventually denied and she was given two-hour, supervised visitation per week with her children.

These court cases and other legal battles involving lesbian mothers become interwoven with academic discourses about lesbian mothers to create hegemonic visions of family, motherhood, lesbianism, and lesbian motherhood. Lesbian mothers themselves are strongly influenced by these hegemonic constructs. However, their experiences are not fully determined by these constraints; rather, their stories of daily life reveal complex mixtures of restraint and autonomy. Forty lesbian mothers' stories are presented throughout this book to illustrate these processes. The next chapter provides details about those who participated and how their stories were collected.

Chapter 2

Eliciting Stories
of Lesbian Parenting

Data for this book come from intensive two-hour interviews conducted with forty self-identified lesbian mothers. An open-ended, unstructured interview approach encouraged respondents to narrate personal stories about important aspects of their parenting experiences. Respondents were also provided with a short story about lesbian motherhood prior to the interview as a strategy for instigating the interview conversation. The short autobiographic story (Martin, 1998) related a lesbian mother's personal experiences as a previously married woman with two teenage children who fell in love with a woman, divorced her husband, and moved away from her exhusband and children to be with her new lover and her lover's daughter. Martin's story was useful for opening the interview dialogue, because it related a number of (mostly sequential) events or story lines that contain themes that applied to a variety of different lesbian-mothering experiences.

While designing this unique approach, I recognized that no single story could possibly capture the diversity of stories expected among the targeted respondents. However, I anticipated that the respondents' similarities and differences from the story would serve as a useful starting point to begin the interviews. Furthermore, from a methodological perspective, it provided consistency across interviews.

Respondents were mailed the short story (and consent form) prior to the interview. They were asked to note any similarities or differences between the author's experiences and their own while reading

Lesbian Motherhood: Stories of Becoming
© 2007 by The Haworth Press, Inc. All rights reserved.
doi:10.1300/5922_03

the story. They were also asked to consider how they might compose their own lesbian motherhood story. These questions served as the starting point for the face-to-face interview.

The cover letter for these materials and the recruitment literature disclosed my background as an unmarried, coupled heterosexual woman with no children. My heterosexuality has made me somewhat of an anomaly among lesbian motherhood researchers; most are lesbian mothers who chose the topic because it resonated with their own personal experiences (e.g., Weston, 1991; Lewin, 1993; Nelson, 1996; Wright, 1998). Lesbian mothers who conduct studies about lesbian motherhood sometimes argue that this gives them a unique sensitivity to the topic due to their insider status. For example, Weston (1991) acknowledged both the positive and negative implications of her own lesbian identity when interviewing gays and lesbians about their kinship experiences. She reported that her lesbian identity facilitated recruitment and established trust and rapport with her respondents. "Many participants mentioned that they would not have talked to me had I been straight, and one or two cited 'bad experiences' of having had their words misinterpreted by heterosexual researchers" (Weston, 1991, p. 14). However, she also admitted that her insider perspective may have resulted in the loss of some details, as respondents left out descriptive background information that they assumed she already knew based on her knowledge and experiences as a lesbian.

My own interest in lesbian motherhood began with the rather mundane experience of writing a term paper for a Sociology of Family course in the mid-1990s. At that time, there was little information available about the experiences of lesbian mothers. This initial term paper evolved into an interview pilot project with nine lesbian mothers (Hequembourg & Farrell, 1999). The stories shared by those women were so powerful and compelling that I was driven to learn more. The current manuscript is a culmination of many years of graduate work as a sociologist. The generosity and candidness of the respondents who participated in the interviews for this book have forever changed my personal politics as well as my career trajectory.

I was always forthright about my personal background while recruiting and networking in the local GLBT communities. However, it's impossible to measure the impact of my outsider status on the recruitment process or interview outcomes. Similar to other heterosexual researchers examining gay and lesbian issues (e.g., McClennen, 2003), I took certain steps to minimize the limitations imposed by my outsider status. My initial interview project with nine lesbian mothers (Hequembourg & Farrell, 1999) provided an opportunity to interact on a personal basis with a number of lesbian mothers with very diverse life stories. I also attended various community events (e.g., Pride parades, book signings, support groups, etc.) that allowed me to meet people in the local gay and lesbian community. Several of my lesbian mother friends helped me make connections in the community and provided me with valuable insights as I planned my methodological strategy. Overall, the respondents in this study indicated that they valued my outsider perspective, because they thought it might give me greater objectivity. In the final analyses, their stories were similar enough to those elicited by insider researchers to indicate that my outsider status did not drastically alter their responses. However, it is possible that the respondents' stories were framed in particular ways for my benefit. Unfortunately, I can do little but acknowledge the possibility because there were no formal means of measuring the impact of my outsider perspective.

THE PROCEDURE

Data were collected during two- to three-hour-long unstructured, open-ended interviews with forty self-identified lesbian mothers ranging in age from twenty-two to sixty-two (Table 1 in Appendix). The average number of children among the respondents was 1.5, although one family had seven children and another, four. Their children ranged in age from unborn to thirty years old. Participation was not limited to a certain definition of "mother" (i.e., biological motherhood, legal motherhood, step-motherhood, and so on); instead, the sample includes women with a variety of different social, legal, and biological relationships to their children.

Among the forty women, twenty had been previously married before coming-out. Predictably, then, nearly half of the women (nineteen) had their children during a prior heterosexual marriage. In addition, one mother (Heidi) deliberately became pregnant after a one-night stand with a man; another (Victoria) was raped and became pregnant. These women will be referred to simply as "birth mothers."

Five other women had become partners with women who had children during prior heterosexual marriages. These women will be referred to as "stepmothers." Two couples conceived via artificial insemination from unknown donors. The birth mother will be referred to as the "biological AI parent" and their partners will be referred to as "coparents." Both of the coparents in the study had legal second-parent rights. Hester, for example, was the birth mother of her five children from a previous marriage and also the comother to her ex-partner's biological child. Another couple had both birth children and foster children in their family. Kim and Mirisa were the legal guardians for their siblings' children; Pearl "step-parented" Kim's nieces. As a couple, Lucille and Becky internationally adopted their two sons (Lucille was legal parent initially, and Becky subsequently obtained legal second-parent adoption of their sons), while Kelly and Maureen domestically adopted their son and daughter (Kelly was the legal parent initially, and Maureen later became the legal second-parent). These women will be referred to as "adoptive mothers," and the legalities of their parental status will be specified when appropriate. I use these terms "stepmother," "birth mother," "coparent," "biological AI mother," and "adoptive mother" only for the sake of clarity, because there is little consensus among the respondents or in the literature as to what the definitive terms might be.

All the women were recruited from an area about 100 miles in radius within Western New York State. Respondents were contacted through a variety of channels: word-of-mouth, newspaper ads, signs in community stores, community professionals including a lawyer and a GLBT agency, and online listserves. In accord with Brown's (1995) definition of "lesbian," I chose to include all those who self-identified as "lesbian." Brown (1995) defines "lesbian" as multi-defined and dependent on a researcher's explanatory models and the parameters of his or her theory or research. She (1995, pp. 9-10) defines lesbian as

> . . . a woman whose primary sexual and affectional attractions are to other women and who has a sexual minority identity, that is, recognizes through the use of language or symbolic expression that her sexual orientation places her apart from a sexual mainstream, even though she may not use the term "lesbian" *per*

se. [. . .] Overt sexual expression of lesbian identity is not required, only that any such expression if it occurs be primarily invested in women. In addition, women who have related to men, and some who continue to relate to men sexually and affectionally, are not necessarily excluded from this definition, depending on the position in which such heterosexual behavior is placed. What is core to this definitional model is that the lesbian sees her relationship and connections to women as *primary,* whether acted upon or not, and identifies herself as outside the sexual mainstream.

I chose this method of selection with full knowledge that the categories we use in our research are neither fixed nor stable in any way. Therefore, I stress the notion that the category of lesbian mothers is not a stable or reified category. Although I have used this term for recruitment purposes, I am not implying that there is anything universal or stable about lesbian mothers as a group. I want to avoid the pitfalls of the existing literature on lesbian motherhood and avoid making the "leap from the empirical presence of relational identities to their *normative* valorization" (Somers, 1994, p. 611, author's italics). Instead, this study will contest and challenge those very categories. The identities that emerge in the women's stories are a "multiplicity of historically varying forms of what are less often unified and singular and more often fractured identities" (Ibid.). Furthermore, to use Margaret Somers' (1994, p. 622) words, this book implicitly assumes that "*all* identities [. . .] must be analyzed in the context of relational and cultural matrices because they do not 'exist' outside those complexes." In short, my emphasis on "lesbian mothers" or "lesbian women" does not imply some underlying authenticity that will be revealed in the course of the study.

A little over half of the women (twenty-four) were interviewed as a couple and the remaining (sixteen), individually. Interviews, conducted in women's homes and local restaurants and cafes, were taped and later transcribed verbatim. Copies of transcripts were supplied to the respondents for their approval. Almost all the respondents were satisfied with the outcomes and made no changes, although one couple did request small changes to their transcribed interview in order to more fully disguise their identities. The transcribed interviews were then loosely coded, and recurrent themes were noted.

Although there is a recognized need to capture the demographic diversity of lesbian and gay families (Patterson, 1995), the difficulty of reaching this hidden population compelled me to widen my scope of inclusion to include any self-identified lesbian with one or more children. Overall, my sample is rather homogenous in terms of social class and race. Similar to most studies of lesbian motherhood (Lewin, 1993; Wright, 1998; Nelson, 1996; Dunne, 2000; Dalton & Bielby, 2000), this sample predominately consists of white, middle-class, well-educated women. Women-of-color and working-class women were underrepresented although there were a few exceptions. Thirty-five of the women were white, two African-American, one African-American/Hispanic, one Native American/Portuguese, and one white/Chippewa Indian. Two women self-identified as working class, nine were lower-middle class, twenty were middle class, and nine self-identified as upper-middle class.

Unlike many other studies that focus on those women who live in urban areas, this sample also consists of women living in suburban and rural residences: twenty-four of the women lived in urban areas, ten lived in suburban areas, and six lived in rural areas of Western New York.

Women worked as academics, schoolteachers, social workers, artists, and administrators. Some were full- or part-time students, retired, or disabled. A bus driver, a machinist, a phlebotomist, a library clerk, a clinical manager, a computer programmer, a legal advocate, an attorney, a chemical technician, two registered nurses, a physician's assistant, a dietician, an accountant, and an engineer were also in the group.

There were several religious backgrounds represented among the respondents. Eleven women identified their religious preference as none; four were Presbyterian, one former Evangelical Christian, one pagan, four Christians, ten Catholics, two "spiritualists," one Catholic/Presbyterian, one Unitarian/Wiccan, two Unitarians, one Muslim, one Unitarian, and one Pentecostal.

Five of the women were single, thirty-one of the respondents lived with their current partners, and four are dating but do not live with their partner. Twelve of these women had been together for ten or more years, five for five or more years, and seventeen for less than five years. One couple has been together for twenty-eight years.

Eighteen of the women had commitment ceremonies with their current partners.

This sample of women is not unbiased and should not be understood as representative of all lesbian mothers. As Arlene Stein (1997, p. 6) pointed out in her study of lesbian identities, "representative samples of stigmatized populations are impossible to obtain; this is perhaps doubly true for groups such as lesbians whose statistical contours are unclear and who do not agree among themselves on the criteria for membership." Like other studies of lesbians, in general, and lesbian mothers, in particular, this sample is predominately white, middle class, and well educated. Consequently, women of color and working-class women are underrepresented. The conclusions that I reach are bounded by these constraints.

Stating such disclaimers is simultaneously necessary and also completely irrelevant. On one hand, conventional sociological methodology requires such disclaimers. However, to make such a disclaimer assumes that generalizability or representativeness is attainable. To obtain a statistically representative sample in sociological terms, a researcher must assume that there is some commonality among all respondents. It is my purpose to deconstruct this notion of commonality and present a portrait of lesbian motherhood that recognizes only shifting alliances that are combined with contradictory lines of flight that destroy, disrupt, and/or undermine those perceived alliances. Consequently, it seems counterintuitive to make claims to generalizability. Another potential reminder for the reader is that, although I address the strategies employed by the respondents, I did not measure or observe their actual practices but only their stories about these practices. Consequently, the data for this paper consist of narrative accounts that are not entirely independent of practice, but by no means identical to practice.

THE COMMUNITIES

The women in this study were interconnected in complex ways with their own social environments. It is beyond the scope of this book to provide a detailed account of the larger, local communities in which these women live their daily lives. However, it is possible to provide some details about their social climates.

Unlike many of the existing studies (Lewin, 1993; Weston, 1991; Nelson, 1996) that were located in progressive urban areas that featured a large and visible gay and lesbian population, respondents in this study were recruited from two midsized Northeastern cities and surrounding areas with smaller, less visible, and less politically oriented gay and lesbian communities. Augustia and Midland (pseudonyms) are located about seventy-five miles from one another. The largest concentration of respondents resided in Augustia or its surrounding suburban areas. The Midland metro population was slightly larger than Augustia in 1999, and the two cities are quite different in their socioeconomic status, with Augustia employing more workers in white-collar service and retail jobs and Midland employing more workers in blue-collar manufacturing jobs. Their per capita incomes for 1990s were similar although Augustia had a substantially lower unemployment rate than Midland.

Midland and Augustia both contain large universities and a number of smaller colleges. Like many college towns, these cities support numerous environmental, political, and social groups; food cooperatives; bookstores; movie houses; bars and nightclubs; restaurants; and small businesses. Each city supports a local gay and lesbian newspaper and several GLBT community service provider organizations. Each city also holds annual Pride events with parades and related activities. Upon attending these Pride events, I found that they were extremely family-friendly events, featuring family picnics and children story-hours. Augustia also supports an organization called "Augustia Dykes" which has several hundred members. This group had an active online constituent and held weekly meetings in local coffee shops. Several of the women in the sample belonged to this group. Midland had several informal groups for lesbian women, although the majority of the group activities available in the metro area catered to the gay male population.

One surprising characteristic of both the cities was the lack of any support groups for lesbian mothers at the time of study. With the ever-increasing visibility of lesbian women with children, this was surprising and disappointing because it would have been a valuable recruitment resource.

One big difference between the two cities was their religious communities. In Midland, there were only a couple of community churches that welcomed membership from the GLBT community. However, Augustia had a very large and active GLBT spiritual community. Many of the respondents were active members of either a gay-friendly church, or they had openly joined their own local congregation.

Women in the study generally felt accepted in their local communities, particularly in Augustia. Most of the respondents were embedded in daily social networks that had nothing specifically to do with their lesbianism (e.g., bars, political organizations, bookstores, etc.). Instead, they belonged to small enclaves of friends who met because they had a particular interest in common (e.g., spiritual reasons and meeting prospective partners were the two big reasons mentioned by the respondents). Some spoke of how parenting became a popular topic of discussion in their friendship groups but it was rarely the primary impetus for their involvement. Only a couple of these women were involved in what they defined as political organizing. However, despite this lack of formal interest in politics, most of them expressed awareness that they lived in communities with fairly progressive legislation policies.

Among the forty women, only three of them had ever experienced a direct threat to the custody of their children due to their lesbianism. Two of these women actually lost custody to their exhusbands. Both women related painful experiences of blatant homophobia in the legal process resulting in the loss of custody of their children. One of these women was able to appeal the decision and had recently regained custody of her young son. Despite these exceptions, the other women reported positive attitudes about their interactions with the legal system. Some of this optimism may have had to do with the surprisingly large number of them who had extremely amiable relationships with their exhusbands. There were also numerous satisfied reports about interactions with the legal system among the group of women that gave birth or adopted while in a lesbian relationship. The majority of the participating coparents had successfully sought second-parent adoption. The ease by which these women acquired second-parent status reflects progressive legal policies in this area of the country.

Several of the women from Augustia specifically expressed contentment with their local communities. One woman told of her fears about her upcoming move to a new city, because she feared that it would not be as "accepting" as Augustia. Another woman felt that

Augustia was more GLBT-friendly than another city where friends resided:

> A friend of ours—he and his partner adopted a little boy and they went down to [a city in another part of New York State] for their pride picnic. His partner's brother was organizing it and they went down and they were shocked. First of all, the size was a lot smaller than the one here in Augustia. And it was all the extremists. There weren't any of the mainstream. In Augustia, it's mostly mainstream and less extremist. He said that he and his partner walked around with their son and everyone looked at them like there was something wrong with them. And here [. . .] there are tons of families.

Hillary, a comother from Augustia, explained how she had spent her early adult years searching for a community in which she could comfortably raise a family without hiding her relationship with her partner. She explained how she had searched for that place before moving to Augustia ". . . because I kept telling Vicky [i.e., her partner] that I'm convinced that it is out there, I just don't know where." I asked her to clarify what she meant by "it" and she responded,

> A lifestyle where you could live together and be a family and not be conceived or considered as something unusual. Not someone like those people marching in the parades, carrying the banners and waving the flags and being, you know, *not* what we were. There had to be someplace where you could still be normal. And I kept convincing myself that it was somewhere. And when I moved to Augustia, I had no idea of the environment that it is. It is very, you know, very comfortable here. *Incredibly* comfortable. And it's well received and it's respected. I don't know if it is because it is such a high white-collar, well-educated area or whether it's because I don't know. I have no idea. But it definitely is. There is no question.

It is beyond the scope of this book to address exactly what makes Augustia different or preferable to other gay and lesbian communities. However, it is worth noting that despite equal recruitment efforts aimed at both cities, more women (approximately 75 percent) responded from the Augustia area. Several respondents hypothesized that Midland's gay and lesbian community was more close-knit and cautious or suspicious of strangers compared to Augustia.

The respondents' social locations and their personal biographies are at the heart of this manuscript. However, their stories do not stand alone. Their parenting experiences are located within a network of interlocking and connected discourses about motherhood and sexuality. Chapter 3 provides a language for a better understanding the processes that link the women's stories with complex institutional structures.

Chapter 3

Analyzing Lesbian Mothers' Subjectivities

Our academic understandings of lesbian motherhood have been strongly influenced by the resistance/assimilationism paradigm. Poststructuralist efforts to better understand the fluidity and multiplicity of subjectivity often fail to make the practical leap between theory and people's everyday experiences. Efforts to understand people's stories about their lived experiences from a poststructuralist perspective are badly needed. The goal of this chapter is to provide a rudimentary understanding of one such framework in order to apply it to the parenting stories of the women participating in this study. Gilles Deleuze's and Felix Guattari's (1987) conceptual tools are utilized to understand how lesbian mothers' subjectivities are not *completely* constituted by normalizing discourses, nor are they radical examples of resistance.[1] It is my hope that such an approach can offer the tools for analyzing other seemingly mundane life experiences and shed light on new ways to think about ourselves and our interactions with others in our social world.

In this chapter, I discuss how Gilles Deleuze and Felix Guattari's work can be used to better understand the fluidity and multiplicity that constitute the respondents' experiences as lesbian mothers. At first, their theoretical concepts may seem alien to the current discussion of lesbian motherhood. However, I will show that this theoretical framework, which seems convoluted and jargon-ridden at times, provides a useful vision of subjectivity that captures the fluidity and contradictory nature of subjectivity formation. Analyses in subsequent

Lesbian Motherhood: Stories of Becoming
© 2007 by The Haworth Press, Inc. All rights reserved.
doi:10.1300/5922_04

chapters will utilize these concepts alongside the respondents' narratives of lived experience. One couple's experiences are first used as a means for contextualizing Deleuze and Guittari's concepts.

MONICA AND TERESA:
"JUST 'MOM' AND 'DAD'"

Teresa and Monica raised their three daughters together in a small, rural town outside a modestly sized city in the Northeastern United States. They were both married when they fell in love at work seventeen years ago. After divorcing their husbands, they each shared custody of their children with their exhusbands. Their daughters' fathers maintained close contact and were actively involved in their daughters' everyday lives. In fact, both exhusbands developed close parent-like ties with each other's children. Teresa and Monica proudly described their close relationships with their daughters and their exhusbands, and stressed the centrality of their parenting roles in their lives.

Monica and Teresa believed that their childhood experiences strongly influenced their parenting philosophies. According to Teresa, "we are much more a product of a lot of our own issues more than the lesbian part. It's just how we were brought up." Monica and Teresa's combined parenting philosophies emphasized their normality and similarity to other parents. Their strategy revolved around a gendered division of caretaking in which Teresa was the "mom" and Monica was the "dad." Teresa commented, "[Our parenting] is a gender thing, too." And Monica agreed,

> She is the mom. I don't think I ever played mom. I am the dad.
> [. . .] And the dynamics that we have to this day are much like
> that: they are gendered. They are typical of what you might hear
> out there about mothers and fathers and their kids and their
> interactions.

When prompted for examples, Teresa responded, "Oh, lots of examples! [. . .] For all girl stuff they come to me." Monica stated, "If they want a jar open, they come to me. Or a project to do." To emphasize her gendered parenting experiences, Monica added, "I don't think I had a real mother experience. [. . .] I could relate to all the fathers." She added that she felt that she knew how to be a successful father, but lacked the skills commonly associated with mothering. Teresa, in contrast, characterized herself as the "female-gender person" and added, "Monica would never want to talk about those kinds of things—[our daughters'] personal issues." They concluded that this made them "such a typical family."

One could interpret Monica and Teresa's parenting philosophies as a form of assimilationism, because they conform to conventional ideologies about parent–child dynamics in the traditional, nuclear, heterosexual family unit. However, their practices are *not* simply reproductions of those ideologies. Instead, their two-mother parenting is unique from conventional understandings of family (i.e., "molar" or institutionalized discourses of family). Their uniqueness could be characterized as a "line of flight" that disrupts conventional definitions of family. Monica and Teresa pride themselves on being "just like any other family," but their experiences do not entirely conform to that dominant ideology. Thus, their parenting experiences, while seeming to be assimilationist, expose the instability of the molar conventional family structure. However, at the same time, their willingness and desire to be perceived as "just another family" flows back to help sustain and validate the stability of ideologies about the conventional family. It is this fluidness and simultaneity of processes that are so interesting about lesbian mothers' experiences. Deleuze and Guattari provide a language to help us better understand these processes.

Deleuze and Guattari propose that we conceptualize subjectivities as "becomings" that are constituted by fluid and multiple lines of movement. Lines of flight are aspects of these movements, comprised of spontaneous bursts of behavior or experience that escape the forces imposed by dominant, constraining powers. Dominant powers congeal in structural manifestations that Deleuze and Guattari refer to as "molar structures." Lines of flight flee from these molar structures and ideologies, but also return to those dominant structures so that both ultimately constitute lesbian mothers' subjectivities. In other words, certain subjectivities coagulate into masses that appear to be stable. These are what we observe to be separate, independent entities called lesbian mothers or lesbian-headed families. Lesbian mothers exist within a constellation of molar structures that seek to define them and make them act in certain ways. An excellent example would be the current political resistance to same-sex marriage. Traditional, heterosexual marriage is a strong molar structure that is employed by conservatives to resist the inclusion of lesbian parents. Despite this ever-increasing resistance to same-sex marriage, lesbian-headed families continue to persevere and thrive. The molar structure of the traditional, heterosexual marriage contrasts with the "molecular" movements instigated by lesbian-headed families. Molecular movements do not fit with molar structural expectations. But, at the same time, they never exist independently of molar structures. Consequently, lesbian mothers pose experiences and practices that move through the system as molecular movements that intersect and disrupt molar structures. At the same time, they also stabilize those molar structures. Lesbian mothers reveal the inconsistency and multiplicity of experience that make up molar structures.

Molar structures are associated with processes by which dominant societal structures are sustained and validated. In "A Thousand Plateaus," Deleuze and Guattari (1987) refer to the processes that sustain molar structures as "reterritorialization." At the same time, the fleeting and unstable molecular movements are associated with processes of "deterritorialization" that disrupt and question molar structures. Brown and Lunt (2002) provide an illustration of the relationship between molar and molecular using an example from social psychology. A group of individuals may appear as a molar structure that is singular, organized, and stable. But the coherence of the group is only derived from the "assembled connections between individuals. [. . .] Switching to the molecular level renders things far more messy and fragmentary than their molar representation might suggest" (Ibid., p. 13).

Processes of deterritorialization and reterritorialization are entirely constituted by power, and can never stand outside power. Everyday practices, like those described by lesbian mothers, are comprised of both deterritorialization and reterritorialization. Some parenting experiences can be conceptualized as micro in nature, because they are fleeting movements that destabilize or deterritorialize molar structures. These are the strategies that are often categorized as resistance by other theorists, because they appear to escape the workings of power to alter ideologies about the traditional family. Other actions work to overcome and prevent these fleeting movements in order to restabilize or reterritorialize molar structures. These lesbian parenting strategies are often defined as assimilationist, because they reinforce existing ideologies of family. However, Deleuze and Guattari's conceptualization of deterritorialization and reterritorialiation reveal a greater complexity of processes than merely resistance and/or assimilation. Instead, lesbian parents are combinations of fleeting and stabilizing movements that never stand outside power. While some practices may appear to disrupt dominant powers, they always return to also reinforce those dominant powers. The disruptions or instability and the stability are simultaneous and cannot exist independently of one another. Deleuze and Guattari (1987) point out the paradox of these processes: strategies employed by subjects to instigate change may work to simultaneously undermine their intentions. A lesbian mother, for example, may want to create her family to avoid heterosexist and gendered expectations that result in the unequal divisions of labor found among many heterosexual household members. Some strategies she employs to avoid these pitfalls may result in more egalitarian relationships in her home. However, her strategies also cannot fully escape the ideological structures upon which the nuclear family is premised. Consequently, the same strategies she employs to promote change also serve to reinforce those ideologies from which she is trying to escape.

From a Deleuzian/Guattarian perspective, this paradox is manageable if one focuses on the instability and promise for ongoing change that accompanies and defines all becomings. There is always the danger of fixating on molar structures that discourage new experience; however, that danger is fleeting, because the opportunities for micropolitical movements are always-already available. Life can therefore be understood as a work in progress that is never simply voluntary or linked to agency (Conley, 2000).

Deleuze and Guattari argue that we can best understand ongoing subjectivity processes through an analytical strategy called "rhizoming." The term "rhizome" comes from botany; it is a type of decentralized root system in plants. The roots of a rhizomic plant grow in unpredictable and spontaneous ways underneath the earth, rather than following the vertical growth pattern commonly found in nature's plants and trees. Deleuze and Guattari employ the concept of "rhizoming" as a strategy or method of analysis and practice to better understand how lines of flight come together to partially constitute molar structures. To rhizome is to make connections rather than trace existing paths. In other words, rhizoming can be used as a conceptual tool to examine the movements that make up lesbian mothers. It allows us to focus on movements or practices rather than being misled into analyzing a fixed and stable lesbian mother Subject. The resulting entity that we see as a lesbian mother is actually a fluid and ever-changing process called a "becoming."

"BECOMING"

"Becoming" is a theoretical construct that can be utilized to understand everyday experience without resorting to conventional notions of a stable, unitary Subject. This new terminology is necessary because, as I've indicated throughout this chapter, subjectivity is fluid and fluctuating, rather than fixed and stable. "Becoming" captures the movement and instability. It suggests that we constantly seek to attain a certain state (i.e., to become something), but yet we never quite achieve that state and, thus, are always becoming. For example, in the upcoming chapters, we will see how the respondents seek a stable sense of self within a societal context that constantly challenges their legitimacy. However, that stable self is always-already elusive and is never attainable. As researchers, we must focus on the processes by which lesbian mothers become constituted through molar and molecular movements. Becoming lesbian mother is *not* a structure or product. Becoming is not about moving from one fixed identity position to a different fixed position. It is not about resisting or assimilating into existing categories. Becoming does not have an ultimate endpoint or a goal that is outside itself.

> Indeed the outcome of any Deleuzean "becoming" is not emphasized, for becoming is a process, a line of flight between states which displaces and disorients subjects and identities. This "betweenness" is experienced, not attained. (Flieger, 2000, p. 43)

Becoming lesbian mother is a process by which transformation brings about a new experience without any sense of an end-goal. It is the experience of the process that constitutes a becoming rather than the beginning or end product upon which we most often focus our research. It requires a shift in focus to see "lesbian mothers" as masses of ever-fluctuating experiences rather than fixed subjects. The experiential process of becoming replaces the fixity of the subject.

Becomings constitute a boundless system of lines of flight that traverse and realign dominant structures. They are always in movement and are never stagnant or at rest. They are alterations from one moment to another where there is no endpoint but only a series of transformative events that constitute all experiences (Grosz, 1994a, p. 204). There is no engineer overseeing these becomings. Sometimes they just happen, but at other times, they are shaped by linkages with surrounding becomings. Consequently, there is room for spontaneity and change but the experience is not under the master control of either the "individual" or those perceived to "hold" power.

> . . . the "being" of each woman is always temporary. An effect of subjectivication, it cannot be separated from a context and is always exceeded by becomings that can neither be completely controlled nor foretold. (Conley, 2000, p. 35)

A becoming allows for constant reinvention, with that reinvention process varying from individual to individual and moment to moment.

Lesbian mothers pose an ideal case study of becoming. They are "always-already" complex combinations of contradictions due to their contested position in our culture. Their experiences are shaped by conservative and traditional ideologies of "family," while also representing exciting innovations. Braidotti (2003, p. 53) points out that lesbian identity is "situated in one of the zones of highest turbulence, at the crest of the wave of exposure and commodification than other brands of sexuality today." However, their uniqueness does not set them entirely apart.

> Lesbians are caught in the same historical contradictions as everyone else: they are simultaneously within and without the majority. The lesbian faces the task of assembling disorganized, monstrously hybrid disruptive bodies, while being simultaneously within the system she is trying to subvert. (Ibid.)

This is precisely why so many researchers are attracted to explanations framed in the resistance/assimilationist debate. However, as I have hopefully demonstrated in my discussion of Deleuze and Guattari's concepts, there are other ways to understand experience that I believe are more perceptive in their ability to capture the (theoretical or conceptual) messiness of lesbian mothers' lived experience. This method is not without its challenges, for it requires us to dispose of a tradition that valorizes the Subject, in exchange for an analytical approach that is unstable and difficult to capture for the purposes of conventional research analysis. This is a topic I will return to throughout the book. First, I return to Monica and Teresa's narrative to illustrate some of these complex processes.

Monica and Teresa's narratives are particularly interesting in light of Monica's insistence on her role as the "dad" in their family. Monica and Teresa embraced the roles of mother and father. This strategy complements American culture's emphasis on the importance of these roles and the cultural centrality of the two-parent (i.e., heterosexual) nuclear families. Ideologies about the superiority of the two-parent, heterosexual nuclear family are encouraged and validated through legal as well as social reinforcements. Mother and father roles exist as the foundation of the idealized, heterosexual family that constitutes our molar understandings of family life. Parenting roles within the ideological nuclear family are seen as two opposites of a whole that only effectively correspond with male/female (male = dad and female = mom). These roles have recently become the foundation for conservative, religious-based movements to limit marriage to a union between a man and a woman. Religious conservatives argue against same-sex marriage, zealously claiming that children's well-beings are at stake. This belief is born of the judgment that only intact, heterosexual nuclear families can raise well-adjusted children. These anti-same-sex marriage discourses attempt to invalidate all other family arrangements.

Monica and Teresa actively linked their roles as mother and father to parenting practices that they associated with these dominant ideologies. However, both of them are *women* so their parenting strategies disrupted the seeming stability of man = dad and woman = mom and highlighted the insufficiency of polarizations that attempt to stabilize these molar categories. Their strategies resulted in an experience of parenthood that relied on predetermined roles, but yet their execution of these roles revealed their inherent instability. The experience of being two mothers who parent as a mother and a father resulted in subjectivities that were in-between the categories encouraged in cultural ideologies. Their experiences relied on these categories while also fleeing from them.

These simultaneous movements of stability and innovation are indicative of the processes by which subjectivities are constituted. If subjectivities are conceptualized as processes of becoming, then Monica and Teresa are always becoming something else. This becoming will never result in the stability that they embraced; rather, the lines of flight that constituted their practices will continue to highlight the instability of their identity categories. This is not to suggest that Monica and Teresa have failed in their attempts to parent. Nor does it suggest that they have done something radically revolutionary or entirely assimilationist. Instead, their narratives reveal the complexity of experience that requires a dynamic understanding of subjectivity rather than one that concretizes those experiences into a stable (or unstable) subject within the assimilationism/resistance perspective. Becoming is the mechanism best suited to accomplish this task.

Other aspects of Monica and Teresa's parenting stories illustrate these processes of becoming. Monica and Teresa had been together for most of their teenage daughters' lives. During this time, they remained in close proximity to their exhusbands who continued to play an active role in the parenting of their children. The importance of biological ties between parents and children became increasingly unimportant as Monica and Teresa's new family developed. Their exhusbands became fathers to all three daughters, irregardless of biological ties. Teresa explained,

> . . . both of their fathers live very close. We stayed right within the same school district that I was in with the little one. Little Monica's father being just in the next school district over. So, the fathers were always there visiting and taking care of [the girls], especially my exhusband when they were later teens in high school [because] Monica was working and I was back in school, so we were *never* home. We would come home very late at night and he always had the responsibility of being there when they got home.

The dynamics that evolved to constitute their family defied the familial connections associated with conventional ideologies of family, even heterosexual blended families. Each of these fathers had no "official" (i.e., biological, legal, or marital) commitment to his ex-wife's partner's children. However, Monica and Teresa's exhusbands never hesitated to include each other's children in their self-stylized families after their divorces. Monica, Teresa, Tim, Bob, and their three daughters formed lasting familial bonds over the years that defied the conventional (biologically and legally defined) family arrangements of tradition. Their chosen family relationships exemplified rhizomatic configurations because their ties to one another posed lines of flight that disrupted the seemingly stable nature of molar structures of family.

Deleuze and Guattari metaphorically describe rhizomes as burrows, which "in all of their functions of shelter, supply, movement, evasion, and breakout" defy linear-based logic systems (1987, pp. 6-7). Rhizomes are assemblages; they are practices constituted by constant becomings. The linkages and connections among Monica, Teresa, their daughters, and the children's biological fathers constituted an assemblage of lines and flows that metaphorically resembled the burrows described by Deleuze and Guattari. Their practices were composed of a variety of movements that held multiple intentions and resulted in varying outcomes. Monica and Teresa's desire to be "just like any other family" was accompanied by practices that, on one hand, *did* make them similar to other families, but, at the same time, made them extremely *different* from other families.

These same lines and flows were disrupted and reterritorialized at other points in their narratives. The relationships among Teresa, Monica, their children, and the children's fathers did not exist outside the molar structures of family that they partially constituted. In fact, the very definition of molar structures rests on their apparent stability and their resistance to disruptions. Molar structures (e.g., family) introduce stabilizing mechanisms into their assemblages in order to avoid losing their specificity (May, 1993b, p. 4). When any form of difference introduces tiny explosions of deterritorialization into the system (e.g., Teresa and Monica's family), the self-binding mechanisms associated with molar structures react. Molar structures seek stability, and therefore react by attempting to suppress the processes of deterritorialization. However, at the same time, these molar structures are inherently unstable and cannot exist independent of the disruptive movements accompanying processes of deterritorialization. "[M]olar unities are the intersection of smaller, molecular lines, upon which they often react back, suppressing or destroying those lines that could prove threatening to them" (May, 1993b, p. 5).

Particular aspects of Teresa and Monica's family life exemplified these lines of flight that disrupted molar unities. Their creation of a family with fluid boundaries that encompassed mothers, children, and exhusbands posed lines of flight that disrupted the molar nuclear family. Their vision of the molar nuclear family was stabilized through a various legal and cultural forces. Because legal and cultural forces continue to exclude same-sex couples from validating their relationships in conventional terms (e.g., marriage, adoption, etc.), Teresa and Monica's family lacked many of these legitimating mechanisms. Monica and Teresa never had any legal ties to each other's daughters, nor have their respective exhusbands ever had any legal ties to the other's children. In essence, their extended family did not exist in the eyes of the law. Lack of recognition introduced various restrictions on their family's practical access to various tangible benefits, such as insurance, social security benefits, child custody, and so on. Mechanisms (e.g., family law) are based on outdated notions of "family" and refuse to acknowledge new family configurations, presumably, in an attempt to stop them from forming or perpetuating. However, as Monica and Teresa's narrative revealed, a lack of legal recognition had very little impact on the way that they defined their family.

Legal efforts are ineffective in dismantling lesbian-headed families, because molar structures of family are partially constituted by lines of flight and would not exist without them. Lesbian-headed families do not exist outside the molar structure called "family," but exist internal to it. In fact, following Deleuzian/Guattarian logic, there are no boundaries around the structure "family." The tiny lines and flows that constitute alternative family forms destabilize these definitions, and rupture their cohesiveness, always-already intersect those very same seemingly unitary and cohesive legal definitions of "family." Conventional legal definitions of family could not exist without lines of flight, such as Monica and Teresa's family practices, because they are defined in contrast to them. Legal discourses attempt to situate lesbian-headed families outside the bounds of family. But, these legal discourses cannot exist without situating themselves in contrast to the "other." Monica and Teresa's narrative illustrates how legal discourses are not separate from alternative practices of family, but they both exist simultaneously within the same system. Thus, the micropolitics of their family exist simultaneously with the macropolitics of the molar heterosexual nuclear family.

Thus far, I have argued that a Deleuzian/Guattarian reading is superior to one that relies on the resistance and/or assimilationist interpretation. Therefore, I would like to provide some examples in the following paragraphs of how one might read Monica and Teresa's narratives through the resistance and/or assimilationist lens in order to illustrate the weaknesses of these approaches.

For example, an assimilationist reading from a legal perspective would centralize the similarities between Monica and Teresa's daily parenting practices and those of heterosexual parents. Such an argument would centralize their ability to successfully fulfill their children's needs through their successful execution of both the mother and father roles. A legal argument based on assimilationism would centralize Monica and Teresa's "normality": their middle-class backgrounds, their economic security, their large network of supportive friends and family, their professional careers, and so on. This perspective would emphasize groups called "families" with clear boundaries around them, which can (and should) be subjected to regulation by the State. Such an interpretation would lead to a very different interpretation of Monica and Teresa's parenting arrangement with their exhusbands. Such a perspective would have to minimize the biological fathers' centrality in the couple's life and relegate them to "helpers," because current legal theory does not allow for more than two parents. Consequently, any attempt to gain legal stepparenting rights for Monica and Teresa would require that their exhusbands' parental roles were minimized and discounted. Their assimilation into conventional categories would be central to such a reading of their experiences.

An assimilationist reading of Monica and Teresa's parenting narratives would unquestioningly accept the rationality of their attempts to normalize and accommodate their "mom" and "dad" identities to existing ideologies surrounding the conventional heterosexual, gendered family structure. The couple invoked strategies that emphasized the stability of their identities through stories of self-progression and realization that simultaneously acknowledged their difference, while also silencing it in exchange for social acceptance. Because Monica and Teresa were so heavily invested in appropriating existing categories and revising them to meet their own needs, they successfully reflected those existing structures. An assimilationist interpretation would suggest that their strategies are ultimately a reflection of existing social structures and pose very little innovation or resistance to those structures.

In contrast, a resistance approach would argue that Monica and Teresa's parenting strategies undermine and alter dominant powers. A resistance perspective would argue that their daily family practices destabilize hegemonic ideologies about motherhood and gender, because they are two *women* who are adopting gendered parenting styles of "mother" and "father." Other lesbian motherhood researchers have argued that the everyday lives of lesbian mothers expose instances of subversion and resistance to patriarchal configurations of family. In Renata Reimann's (1997, p. 157) study of the division of household labor among AI lesbian couples, she predicted that her respondents would "face the unique opportunity and challenge of developing models of parenthood and the division of labor that are independent of gender specific expectations." Independence from gendered expectations assumes that there is an autonomous Subject who can step outside power to resist oppressive gender stereotypes and expectations.

A reading from a resistance perspective might be cautious of the parenting strategies employed by Monica and Teresa that centralize their normality and similarity to other parents. For example, a resistance interpretation might focus on the ways that their strategies ultimately seem to rely on a version of self that strongly reflects existing ideals of the traditional, heterosexual family unit. Although their parenting indicates some uniqueness from existing ideologies of family, motherhood and gender, their foremost parenting strategies are aimed at demonstrating their normality and similarity to existing categories. Thus, their strategies generally reflect and/or reinforce mainstream discourses of lesbian motherhood and motherhood. They recognized the importance of "fitting in," and consequently, they invoked parental strategies that reflected mainstream expectations about parenting.

An interpretation based on a resistance paradigm might argue that Teresa and Monica's parenting practices are dangerous, because they entail the unquestioning embrace and appropriation of oppressive gendered family discourses. Furthermore, daily family life centered on assimilationism mimics conventional family structures in order to be just like any other family (i.e., "normal"). A resistance perspective would conclude that their attempts to assimilate result in practices that are just as tightly interwoven into existing forms of domination as any other family form. Teresa espoused the virtues of forming a two-mother family that emphasized a mother/father structure in their daily interactions. But, then she admitted that this resulted in an inequality in which one of them "steers the boat and the other compromises." Monica and Teresa internalized ideologies of acceptability and made them their own by strongly emphasizing normalization. Consequently, they became trapped by conventional gender stereotypes and subjected to the same oppressions imposed on heterosexual families.

These interpretations of Monica and Teresa's parenting narratives are limited, because they reinforce the polarized emphasis on subversive or assimilationist properties. Polarized interpretations of their narratives fail to capture the fluidity and multiplicity that makes up the lines and flows related to molar and molecular structures. Any multiplicity uncovered through an assimilationism or resistance paradigm is interpreted as a form of diversity that reflects back to one center, namely, the heterosexual nuclear family. They pose a difference from that traditional family form, but ultimately their strategies return to that center. Consequently, there is very little sense of multiplicity and fluidity within their narratives when we employ such a method of analysis. Furthermore, this interpretation assumes that Monica and Teresa are Subjects who negotiate inside or outside power mechanisms to accomplish their goals. It implies that they hold the autonomy to make decisions that result in strategies that are either forms of resistance or assimilation. Social structures and their oppressive results are acknowledged, but only as pressures that are exerted on them as autonomous individuals.

A Deleuzian/Guattarian reading asks a different question and comes up with a very different answer than resistance and assimilation perspectives. Deleuzian/Guattarian attempts to capture the fluidity and multiplicity of subjectivity would ask, "When a lesbian mom behaves in a certain way to gain social acceptance, what is she doing?" This question emphasizes the process of becoming rather than focusing on a stable lesbian mother Subject. It understands that lesbian mothers are not entities in and of themselves, but are only relations of movements that congeal and dissolve in ongoing processes of becoming. Their movements bring them "in contact" with molar ideologies and structures that sometimes capture their becomings in macropolitical mechanisms, but their becomings also involve spontaneous lines of flight that flee those molar structures and reveal their instability. This conceptualization of subjectivity emphasizes the impossibility of separating assimilationism and resistance into different strategies. However, it is more than simultaneity, because the concepts themselves lose their decisiveness when placed within this analytical framework. Resistance suggests the possibility of moving outside a structure, while assimilationism suggests adapting difference into sameness within the structure. According to Deleuze and Guattari, there is no outside and inside so the two concepts lose their specificity and are subsumed into processes of "becoming." From a Deleuzian/Guattarian standpoint, it's not possible to understand lesbian motherhood strategies from an assimilationist or resistance perspective, because these approaches "[rely] on binary logic to describe phenomena of an entirely different nature" (Deleuze & Guattari, 1987, p. 11). Lesbian mothers are never merely assimilationists or resistors and to suggest so would be a misguided attempt to reconcile two phenomena of entirely different natures.

In order to understand lesbian mothers' experiences as ongoing processes, we must reject philosophical traditions that define subjects as compilations of accumulated experiences. As we will see from the respondents' parenting narratives throughout the remainder of this book, their experiences cannot be reduced to tidy, definable accumulations of experiences. Instead, lesbian mothers are constellations of practices and experiences that are always-already in process. Lesbian mothers can be conceptualized as constant foldings and unfoldings of experiences. There are no fixed centers to these malleable constructs; instead, bits and pieces are constantly moving in and out of the folds to become intertwined with other surrounding unfoldings in a "spiraling distributive process" (Semetsky, 2003, p. 217). As Monica and Teresa's narratives illustrated, lesbian mothers cannot be understood as autonomous beings that are either assimilating or resisting the structures that surround them. Instead, they are parts of those structures in a complicated multiplicity of unfoldings that result in fleeting images of fixity that can only be temporarily captured for study. Subjects are, in Judith Butler's words, "a structure in formation" (Butler, 1997, p. 10). All subjects, including lesbian mothers, are both enabled and constrained by the workings of power by which they are constituted. "A power *exerted on* a subject, subjection is nevertheless a power *assumed by* the subject, an assumption that constitutes the instrument of that subject's becoming" (Butler, 1997, p. 11). Lesbian mothers are products of power, but the process by which they come into existence create the opportunity or space for movement within the process of subjectification. In order to understand better the molar structures that shape and are shaped by lesbian mothers, I turn next to a discussion of hegemonic motherhood ideologies.

Chapter 4

Ideologies of Motherhood

Current academic understandings of motherhood would be impossible without feminist insights over the last several decades. Feminists from a wide variety of disciplines have questioned prevalent assumptions about the monolithic nature of the family (Thorne, 1982). Prominent sociologists (Skolnick, 1991; Coontz, 1992, 1997) have confronted popular beliefs about the historical dominance of the nuclear, heterosexual family. Others (Weston, 1991) have challenged the idea that there is anything natural or biologically based about family relationships. The notion of "the family" has been deconstructed to reveal the important role that sex, gender, and age play in familial processes. Feminists have revealed how these structures play an important role in the differentiation of experiences among family members. Dichotomous divisions among public, private, family, and society have resulted in critiques that uncover both the "overprivatization" of family life and also the blurring or dissolution of these boundaries. Perhaps, most importantly, feminist analyses have addressed the insidious ways that power works to enhance patriarchy in and through family relationships. Motherhood stands as a vital component of these academic discussions of family life.

Feminism has widened the choices available to women concerning family and motherhood and, in the process, caused heated public debate concerning the relative value of the different options now open to women. Motherhood continues to be a vastly contested and ideologically laden experience. Lesbian motherhood is one of the most scrutinized and controversial of these experiences. Consequently,

Lesbian Motherhood: Stories of Becoming
© 2007 by The Haworth Press, Inc. All rights reserved.
doi:10.1300/5922_05

lesbian motherhood poses promising terrain for understanding lingering ideologies about motherhood and the consequences of those ideologies for all women.

ESSENTIAL MOTHERHOOD

Motherhood is biologically inscribed, but also heavily influenced and shaped by social and cultural factors (Glenn, 1994). The majority of all women will experience motherhood at some time in their lives, but their experiences are shaped by race/ethnicity, age, sexual orientation, marital status, and socioeconomic status. Despite the highly diversified nature of mothering experiences, American culture contains a particularly narrow ideology of motherhood to which all women are held accountable (whether or not they mother). Patrice DiQuinzio (1999, p. xiii) refers to the quintessential ideology of motherhood as "essential motherhood." Essential motherhood ideologies assume that mothering is a central function of women's female nature (DiQuinzio, 1999). These ideologies presume that motherhood is inevitable and natural. Women are expected and required to exhibit exclusive and selfless devotion to their children. According to DiQuinzio, essential motherhood ideologies assume that women's psychological and emotional well-beings are dependent on the fulfillment of their innate mothering needs. Women's sexualities, according to essential motherhood ideologies, are defined in terms of their mothering. Mothering is seen as the primary goal of women's sexual desire; women's capacity for sexual pleasure and fulfillment outside procreation is devalued. According to DiQuinzio (1999), essential motherhood ideologies dictate that all women should be mothers and those who do not mother are deviant or deficient. Furthermore, those who fall outside acceptable definitions of mothering are devalued. "Essential motherhood is not only an account of mothering, but also an account of femininity" (DiQuinzio, 1999, p. xiii). Men and women are implicated in the perpetuation of these ideologies, although they are rarely explicitly recognized or acknowledged. DiQuinzio points out that the ideologies inherent in essential motherhood are hegemonic, because we take them for granted and rarely question them. Through our embrace of these ideological formations, we overlook the contradictions that manifest themselves in and through their deployments.

Michelle Hoffnung (1998) proposed a similar evaluation of the ideologies using the concept of the "motherhood mystique." Biological, custodial motherhood is presented as the only "natural" path to childrearing and other forms of parenting are ignored or silenced. The motherhood mystique has four aspects (Hoffnung, 1998, p. 282):

> (1) . . . ultimate fulfillment *as a woman* is achieved by becoming a mother; (2) the body of work assigned to mothers—caring for child, home, and husband—fits together in a noncontradictory manner; (3) to be a good mother, a woman must like being a mother and all the work that goes with it; (4) a woman's intense, exclusive devotion to mothering is good for her children.

Lesbian women, like all women, are not immune to the influence of essential motherhood ideologies and the expectations imposed by the motherhood mystique. However, lesbian women's experiences of mothering are considered suspect, because they stand outside the bounds of heterosexuality. Patriarchy and heterosexism have been powerful forces behind this mystique and lesbian women's rejections of sexual relations with men are often perceived as threatening. Mothering without direct interaction with men (especially through alternative insemination) is particularly threatening to patriarchy. Consequently, lesbian mothers fall to the bottom of the "motherhood hierarchy" (DiLapi, 1989).

According to DiLapi's (1989, p. 110) motherhood hierarchy, an "appropriate mother":

> . . . is a heterosexual woman, of legal age, married in a traditional nuclear family, fertile, pregnant by intercourse with her husband, and wants to bear children. She is likely to be able-bodied, or normal mental functioning, of middle- to upper-middle class status, and supported primarily by her husband.

Heterosexism defines the appropriate mother. These ideologies, as a whole, influence the allocation of resources by mainstream institutions (e.g., social service agencies, medical facilities, and legal systems) and dictate where all other mothers fall in the hierarchy.

"Marginal mothers" (e.g., teen mothers, disabled mothers, single mothers, and foster mothers) fail to fulfill the epitome of the ideal mother, because their families do not include a father. "Inappropriate mothers" are the most deficient of all mothers within the hierarchy, because they are not heterosexual. Consequently, lesbian mothers are relegated to the lowest tier of the "motherhood hierarchy" (DiLapi, 1989). Their categorization as "inappropriate mothers," according to DiLapi, is constantly reinstated through power mechanisms in the legal system and academic arena. According to DiLapi (1989, p. 114), the placement of lesbian mothers in the lowest tier of the motherhood hierarchy reflects an attempt to marginalize those women who threaten the social order. The continued subordination of lesbian mothers to the lowest tier of the motherhood hierarchy is perpetuated through the dispersion of various myths regarding their parenting abilities. Lesbian mothers are depicted as unfit parents, because their children have no father figure. Some fear that the children of lesbians will be more likely to grow up gay (as if this is a negative thing). Lesbian mothers are inaccurately depicted as oversexed and likely to molest their children. They are attacked as being too egocentric to provide proper emotional and physical care for their children. Lastly, these myths dismiss all lesbian relationships as unstable and short-lived. These myths are continuously reborn despite empirical evidence to refute them. Their perseverance is indicative of the strength of the motherhood hierarchy and the essential motherhood ideologies that sustain them.

Ellen Lewin's (1993) interviews illustrated how lesbian mothers embrace and sustain essential motherhood ideologies. Lesbian mothers in her study depicted motherhood as the defining event in their lives, thus insinuating the relative inferiority of women who choose not to mother. They minimized and discounted their lesbianism by embracing and centralizing a socially validated motherhood identity.

> ... [M]others tend to downplay the significance of their lesbianism in giving accounts of themselves; instead they speak with intensity of the separation they perceive between themselves and nonmothers and, most hauntingly, of the ways in which motherhood provides them with access to sources of goodness, enabling them to construct a satisfying identity for themselves. (Lewin, 1993, p. 110)

Despite her projection about the similarities between lesbian and heterosexual mothers, Lewin was surprised by the breadth of those similarities and the relative absence of differences reported by the respondents. She hypothesized that the participants in her study emphasized their similarities to other mothers in response to the strength of "good mother" ideologies in our culture. "[T]he narratives of lesbian and heterosexual mothers were similar not necessarily because the women's experiences were comparable but rather in spite of the fact that they may not have been" (Lewin, 1993, p. 11). She concluded that all women are driven by a cultural imperative to achieve motherhood, regardless of sexual orientation. Unfortunately, the acquisition and embrace of these ideologies further perpetuate negative images of nonmothers and create divisions based on parenting experiences. Lesbian mothers, therefore, report positive benefits associated with motherhood at the expense of themselves and all nonmothers. Their acquisition of motherhood benefits also may come at the expense of other aspects of their identities, particularly their lesbianism.

> Gender boundaries are still firmly in place, along with underlying concepts of the "natural," though they have stretched a bit to accommodate a new group of mothers. In this incarnation of reproductive stratification, lesbians are no longer automatically denied access to the system of meanings we call motherhood; rather, they now have the possibility of choosing motherhood [...] and thereby gaining access to womanhood through negotiation. So while this new inscription expands the category of "woman," it does nothing to change the definitions associated with it. Women are still mothers, although heterosexual nonmothers in their childbearing years are perceived more easily than lesbian nonmothers as on the way to becoming mothers or as having suffered a putative loss by not bearing children as they grow older. (Lewin, 1993, p. 115)

As lesbian mothers seek certain ideals about motherhood, they reinscribe essential motherhood ideologies by distancing themselves from others who don't fulfill them, such as lesbians without children (Lewin, 1993). Lesbian women's pursuits of life satisfaction through motherhood are shaped by essential motherhood ideologies, but also play a vital role in perpetuating these ideologies. These processes are transparent in debates surrounding the increasing availability of mothering options among lesbians.

CONTROVERSIES OVER BIOLOGY, MOTHERHOOD, AND FAMILY

Technological and medical advances in the past decade have created a host of new options for couples unable to conceive through heterosexual intercourse. Heterosexual couples comprised the majority of patients seeking these services until the late 1980s. Infertility is a tremendously emotional experience that has traditionally been understood as a "private problem," rarely discussed outside the boundaries of the family. Artificial insemination has traditionally been a taboo topic, particularly when heterosexual couples conceive using an unknown donor's sperm through a sperm bank.

Societal discomfort with donor inseminations among Americans is an artifact of the cultural importance placed on biological ties between parents and children. *USA Today* (Rubin, 2000) reported that donor insemination among heterosexual couples remains a stigmatized practice, with the majority of clients keeping the experience secret from their AI-conceived children and others. The covertness of AI has been encouraged and condoned by doctors for decades. *USAToday* reported that some doctors go to the great length of inseminating potential mothers with a mixture of their husband's sperm and a donor's sperm so that the couple can "focus on the remote possibility that the husband is the father" (Rubin, 2000).

Secrecy about artificial insemination is possible because others assume that the heterosexual couple conceived their child through intercourse. Single women and lesbian women are slowly undermining this culture of secrecy as greater numbers seek AI services (Rubin, 2000). The illusion of biological parenting by heterosexual couples is not an option for lesbian couples who conceive using donor insemination. One indication of the growing trend away from secrecy in AI procedures is a growing number of health agencies offering donor insemination services that release the identity of the donor when the child reaches age eighteen. Reportedly, at the Sperm Bank of California, four-fifths of the patients, most of whom are lesbian couples or single heterosexual women, choose an identity release option.

Despite the great demographic changes among families in the United States (e.g., blended families, single mothers, adoptions, surrogate mothers, and lesbian parents), donor identity release programs sustain a lingering tradition that centralizes biological ties between parents and children. Some lesbian couples with children demonstrate the need to secure their child's rights to access his or her biological father's identity through their selection of donor identity release programs. As more lesbian mothers choose donor insemination programs that allow their children to learn the identity of the donor, they undermine the tradition of silence among heterosexual couples that conceal their use of donor insemination. As *USA Today* (Rubin, 2000) suggests, this practice holds the potential for gradual transformation in many preconceptions still held about alternative insemination practices. However, an unstated implication is that lesbian mothers reinforce the importance of biological ties between children and parents through their selection of these programs. This is a paradoxical strategy, since both mothers are not biologically tied to their children. Lesbian couples facilitating donor identity release programs perpetuate the idea that a child is not complete without knowing his or her biological father—an ideology that is clearly validated among the majority of heterosexual couples using donor insemination who choose not to reveal their child's AI origins.

These couples, whether lesbian or heterosexual, are making their decisions in a cultural context that centralizes biological ties between parents and children. Because biological ties between parents and children commonly result from heterosexual intercourse between a man and a woman, the silence surrounding donor insemination procedures and the desire for identity release programs further reinscribe the motherhood hierarchy and essential motherhood ideologies. While lesbian women have little choice but to reveal their use of donor sperm, their use of donor identity release programs fails to challenge the ideologies associated with parenthood and rooted in biology.

It's not my intention to place judgment on lesbian mothers who choose identity release programs. Instead, I want to point out that the donor identity release programs illustrate the complex ways that seemingly contradictory strategies come together to constitute lesbian mother identities. Strategies like donor insemination seem extraordinarily revolutionary in challenging the power of patriarchal definitions of family. However, at the same time, they reterritorialize those very same patriarchal ideologies. These ideologies then become concretized as molar structures and emerge in and through the narratives of lesbian mothers. Before I turn to specific illustrations of this process among the women in this study, I want to further explore the centrality of biology in our ideologies about parenthood and the impact that these ideological systems have on mainstream discourses about lesbian motherhood.

The emphasis placed on biology in donor insemination practices is not an isolated theme. Turning to other news articles in the popular press, we see an emphasis on biology in other subtle and not-so-subtle ways. For example, a Massachusetts lesbian couple petitioned the court to have both their names on their newborn's birth certificate. Currently, no state allows lesbian couples to place both their names on their child's birth certificate at the time of birth. The birth certificate is typically changed to recognize both legal parents only after second-parent adoption rights are issued by the court. In fact, birth certificate forms do not even provide designations other than "mother" and "father." Thus, biological lesbian mothers are the only legally recognized parent on the form. Nonbiological parents remain invisible until legal second-parent status can be obtained from the courts. This has clear implications for the rights afforded to the child, visa-a-vis his or her nonbiological mother.

When Mary Jane Knoll and Christine Finn asked their hospital to allow them to cross off "father" and replace it with a second category of "mother," the hospital turned to the courts for a decision. This case, however, is unique: Finn gave birth to their child through in vitro fertilization after artificial insemination failed. During the in vitro fertilization process, Knoll's eggs were harvested, fertilized, and implanted into her partner, Finn, who eventually gave birth to their son. Due to the in vitro process, their son is genetically related to Knoll, with Finn as the gestational mother. This situation contrasts with the experiences of the majority of lesbian mothers seeking insemination in North America, whose children are genetically related only to the birth mothers (who are also the gestational mothers), and the other parents have no genetic or legal ties to their newborn infants. In vitro fertilization is less popular, because it is costly, painful, and has a lower success rate. In the case of Finn and Knoll where the infant was genetically related to Knoll and gestationally related to Finn as a result of the in vitro insemination procedure, the courts found in favor of their petition to have Knoll's name listed on the birth certificate as the other parent. The courts indicated the importance of the mothers' ties to their son and their shared intent to raise the child together as grounds for their decision to allow two women as legal parents on a birth certificate. The couple's attorney predicted that this decision might compel other lesbian couples to seek in vitro fertilization in order to circumvent the second-parent adoption process, which she says many couples find to be "oxymoronic."

In Knoll's and Finn's particular case, they were able to change the line on their son's birth certificate from "father" to "mother" to legalize Knoll's nonbiological relationship to her son. Their experiences are indicative of changing ideologies about family in the United States. The court's decision unwittingly undermines the validity of the heterosexual unit as the sole proprietors of legal standing with newborn children. This places the very need for the role of "father" in question. Because essential motherhood ideologies centralize the heterosexual nuclear family unit, lesbian couples who challenge those ideologies face vehement criticisms. Recent public outcries against same-sex marriage and lesbian and gay parenting by the U.S. religious right, illustrate the construction of these ideologies.

The Family Research Institute (FRI), for example, vehemently argues that same-sex marriage should never be instituted in the United States, because marriage is a sacred union between a man and a woman.[1] Their arguments against same-sex marriage are grounded in their religiously inspired condemnation of homosexuality and lesbian and gay parenting. In a 1999 "Family Research Institute Legislative Proposal," FRI specifically calls for an antigay parenting bill that would unequivocally favor the heterosexual parent in custody disputes, and would bar gays and lesbians from legal adoptions, foster parenting, surrogacy, or artificial inseminations.[2] They support this proposed bill with assertions about the dangers of homosexuality, including a propensity to "spread sexually transmittable diseases that are dangerous, burdensome, and costly to society." FRI calls for the prohibition of parenting by gays and lesbians, because "children raised by those who engage in homosexuality are more frequently subjected to a hypersexualized environment, sexual exploitation, rejection by their peers, rejection by adults, and other emotional harm."

FRI's publisher, Paul Cameron, is a well known and controversial critic of homosexuality, same-sex marriage, and gay parenting. In an online pamphlet entitled "Same sex marriage: Till death do us part?" Cameron rallies against same-sex marriage on the basis, among other things, that "homosexuals are poor parents." He cites his own study[3] in support of claims that children raised by gay and lesbian parents are more likely to be dissatisfied children, to experience sexual victimization as children, and to become gay in adulthood, compared with children raised by heterosexual parents. Paul Cameron's work has been vastly criticized; he was dropped from membership in the American Psychological Association in 1983 and was the topic of a resolution denouncing his research by the American Sociological Association in 1985. However, as Gregory Herek, professor of Psychology at the University of California at Davis, points out,[4]

> Lacking training in research methods and statistics, however, nonscientists may not be equipped to subject the Cameron group's results to the rigorous scrutiny that they warrant. Consequently, they may mistakenly assume that the Cameron group's papers are basically sound because they included lengthy bibliographies, reported many statistics, and were published in academic journals. Some members of the lay public may not understand that the mere presence of bibliographic references does not guarantee an assertion's accuracy or validity, that statistics can easily be generated from faulty data, and that academic journals vary widely in their quality and their criteria for accepting papers for publication.

Criticisms of same-sex marriage and gay parenting articulate a variety of common concerns (and misconceptions) about the well-being of children raised by lesbian mothers. Discourses against same-sex marriage and gay parenting highlight some of the complex ways that discourses about lesbian motherhood are articulated in and through various concerns about family, motherhood, and marriage in Western culture. Rooted in extremist religious views, these discourses nonetheless are representative of many mainstream movements to limit the parenting and marital rights of gays and lesbians. Critics assert that childbearing is a privileged act conducted only between consenting adult heterosexual men and women. A common concern is that children of lesbian couples will be disadvantaged or harmed, because they lack a father-figure. Paul Cameron's work at FRI goes so far as to characterize these family arrangements as unhealthy and dangerous. These myths help perpetuate the motherhood hierarchy (DiLapi, 1989) and sustain heterosexist family ideologies that are realized through social structures such as the legal system.

Understandably, lesbian-headed families are particularly sensitive to these criticisms and are often forced to defend their families against such attacks. In an article covering the annual gathering of gay and lesbian families in Provincetown, Massachusetts, one gay father was quoted as saying, "It's a thing we hear a lot. Are you damaging a child because she has two homes, or two dads or two moms? Stuff like that is so ground into our society that whenever we see evidence of healthy teenagers in such families, it's encouraging."[5] This fear is particularly difficult for gay and lesbian parents to address when it comes from their own families of origin. In an article in *The Toronto Star,*[6] a lesbian woman's mother describes her reaction to her daughter's decision to have a child with her lesbian partner, "Oh my God, now they are going to bring a child into this."

This grandmother's concern over the birth of her grandson is not uncommon among heterosexual parents of same-sex couples. "I stopped dead in my tracks. I told her cancer would be easier to understand." Lesbian motherhood remains a vastly contested and misunderstood experience in contemporary society, according to *The Toronto Star* account: "Society is not kind to same-sex couples. Why ask a little child to share that burden? Won't a child suffer without a parent of the opposite gender? Isn't it likely the grandchild will grow up gay or lesbian, too?"

Concerns about the impact of parental homosexuality on children became the center of debate in a 2001 Florida court decision upholding laws against adoption or foster parenting by gays and lesbians. The heated nature of these debates became particularly evident in a talk show aired by a major news channel on June 13, 2001. Guests of the show included well known public figures in the debate: the plaintiff in the Florida case, Doug Houghton; his attorney, Leslie Cooper;

Robert Knight, a vocal critic of lesbian and gay families and member of Concerned Women for America; Armstrong Williams, a critic of lesbian and gay families from Talk American Radio Network; Alan Amberg, founder of Lesbigay Radio; Richard Hatch, a gay father who recently gained notoriety as the winner of a popular reality series; and Meema Spadooa, a documentary producer who was raised by a lesbian couple. Their exchanges illustrate the issues at stake in these debates. On one side, Robert Knight spoke out against lesbian and gay families. He argued vehemently against any legalized endorsement of gay or lesbian parenting, because he believed that same-sex parenting was inherently damaging to children's psychological well-being. His condemnation of same-sex parenting was centered on his belief that children will flourish only when they have a mother and father as role models.

> And it's only been recently that we've said, gee, it doesn't seem to matter whether a child has a mother and father, two fathers are the same as having a mother and father, or two mothers are the same as having a mother and father. I think audience members ought to ask themselves if their fathers could be replaced by a lesbian lover and they would notice the difference, or if their mothers played so—played so little a role in their development that it wouldn't have made any difference to them if their father had been kissing a male lover instead. This is not reasonable to assume that men and women are interchangeable like automobile parts. I mean, men and women [bring] very special— very unique things to a relationship.

> I think sexuality is important and so do you. Otherwise, you wouldn't be announcing you are an openly gay man. Sexuality is a large part of who we are, and kids know that: they watch for clues about how to behave. They know that men and women are built for each other, and they know that there is something wrong when they see two men kissing.

Similar to the religious rhetoric described earlier in this chapter, Knight centralizes the importance of mothers and fathers in families and essentializes the combination of masculine and feminine traits that he feels best epitomize good parenting. From his vantage point,

sexual intercourse between men and women is "natural" and, therefore, only heterosexual parents provide "healthy" outcomes for children. Some e-mail contributors and audience members echoed his
sentiments:

> If I had to give a child up for adoption, I would want the best
> family possible, but I can't believe that a homosexual couple
> could provide that. It makes me wonder why people who want
> to be parents would choose relationships that have no possibil-
> ity of childbearing.

> Well, actually, the only problem I see is by their choice of sexual
> preference they have excluded the possibility of having kids
> naturally. So, really, they have already decided that they don't
> want kids, you know.

> Such an idea is totally unfair to children. It warps their view of
> what is normal.

Armstrong Williams, another critic of same-sex parenting on the
talk show, contributed his own insights into the harm done when public policy endorses lesbian and gay parents. Williams' argument centered on morality and what he perceived to be the inability of lesbian
and gay parents to teach their children proper moral virtues.

> . . . love is not enough to raise a child. It's like love is not enough
> to sustain a marriage. And what a child needs for his mental
> spiritual nurturing is that they need stability. They need guide-
> lines. They need principles, they need values, on which to live
> by, and to guide their lives, in order to make decisions. This is
> really an issue about morality. [. . . Gay parenting . . .] is not the
> moral example, as far as I'm concerned, that you'd want a child
> to emulate. I think in the end that child may feel loved and the
> parents could do a very good job for that child, but that child is
> confused, especially about his moral compass, about his own
> moral character. And also, to try and explain that he has two
> mommies, or explain that he has two daddies. [. . . .] But my atti-
> tude is homosexuals have a right to not be discriminated against.
> I'm tolerant. I have to love and accept all people. But when you
> put a child in that household, that foundation is already flawed.

And yes, good can come from that child, but that child will never be complete. That child will always be sort of rudderless in life without that moral compass.

Underscoring William's words was self-righteousness about what constitutes "morality." His measure of morality was upheld through reference to the need for heterosexual nuclear families. Fear of the homosexual contagion was apparent in his words. He claimed that he is "tolerant," and his dislike for lesbian and gay parenting is a moral issue rather than a personal or political one.

It is little wonder that those who wish to defend the social liberties of lesbian often turn to academic research to support their claims when faced with such harsh criticism of lesbian parenting. In this particular talk show debate, findings from academic research were cited on numerous occasions to show that children experience few, if any, ill effects from being raised by lesbians and gays. Interestingly, however, Richard Knight employed Stacey and Biblarz's (2001) recent findings as a rationale for denying lesbian and gay parenting rights.

As you will recall from Chapter 1, Stacey and Biblarz (2001) reviewed the existing literature about childhood outcomes in lesbian and gay families. Their findings suggested that researchers were overlooking the strengths of diversity in lesbian and gay families by centralizing the similarities among children raised by lesbians, gays, and heterosexuals. They suggested that emphasis on similarity over difference in research about childhood outcomes has been strategically chosen, because it offers credible support for political movements to attain equality for GLBTs. Interestingly, their own work has often been appropriated by critics of gay and lesbian families, such as Richard Knight, a participant on the talk show about same-sex parenting. Stacey and Biblarz's (2001) publication was risky, but also courageous, because they dared voice a controversial perspective about a heated topic.[7] Unfortunately, any scholarly report that hints at differences in childhood outcomes becomes a potential weapon against lesbian and gay families. Most researchers focus on the similarities between lesbian families and other families rather than the differences to avoid these dangers. Jacqui Gabb (2001, p. 345) insightfully notes the consequences of these well-intentioned studies: "It seems that to muddy the familial waters is far too risky: the lesbian family must be sanitized" (Gabb, 2001, p. 345).

Criticisms of lesbigay families are deployed in an attempt to further hegemonize conventional ideologies of family. As a result of these discursive practices, the inherently unstable molar ideologies associated with "the family" are stabilized. Thus far, I have located discourses about lesbian mothers within larger discursive spaces centered on family and motherhood. These discursive spaces disguise the workings of power in ways that attempt to desexualize the family. Essential motherhood ideologies assume heterosexuality, and lesbian mothers are relegated to the lowest tier of acceptability in the motherhood hierarchy (DiQuinzio, 1999; DiLapi, 1989). On one hand, legal discourses centralize heterosexuality as the norm and, consequently, single-out lesbian mothers for special consideration due to their difference. However, at the same time, the legal system commonly employs the nexus approach (i.e., a legal approach that dictates that sexuality has no bearing on one's ability to parent) in an attempt to avoid biased rulings. Lesbian mothers themselves attempt to dismiss their own sexual differences as a factor in their ability to parent. These multiple levels of dialogue about biological primacy in family relationships perpetuate heterosexism. These discourses illustrate a strong polarization in our culture that either denies lesbian mothers' access to the privileged category of "family" and "motherhood" or supports their assimilation into those categories. These polarizations reinscribe the taken-for-granted binaries that underpin heterosexual ideologies. In the following chapters, I propose an analytical strategy using Deleuze and Guattari's concepts that avoid these polarizations and, instead, focus on the simultaneity of micropolitics and macropolitics and the processes of becoming that come to constitute the subjectivities of the forty lesbian mothers participating in this study.

Chapter 5

Lines and Flows
of Lesbian Motherhood

In the previous chapters, I discussed the articulation of parenthood, lesbian motherhood, and family ideologies in legal, academic, and popular discourses. The macropolitical implications of these discourses become evident in the narratives of the forty respondents in this study. Their narratives of motherhood are generated and constituted in and through molar structures of motherhood and the lines of flight that deterritorialize motherhood discourses and practices. In this chapter, I explore how the respondents grapple with the intersection between their sexuality and their mothering experiences. I examine how they instigate strategies of normalization, which eventually fragment as a result of the intensities and flows that intersect the molar categories that (fail to) define them. I end the chapter with Hillary and Vicky's story about their parents' reaction to their decision to parent in order to show the fluidity of becoming processes and the multiplicity of interlocking becomings that emerge within their story.

THE (NON)INTERSECTIONALITY
OF LESBIANISM AND MOTHERHOOD

Monica and Teresa were introduced in Chapter 3 as the couple who parented as "mom" and "dad." An important aspect of their parenting strategy was their resolute detachment of their lesbianism from their motherhood. Teresa stated, "That's the hard part about

Lesbian Motherhood: Stories of Becoming
© 2007 by The Haworth Press, Inc. All rights reserved.
doi:10.1300/5922_06

describing *lesbian* motherhood—it has just been *motherhood*." Many of the respondents indicated that their experiences as mothers over-shadowed their lesbianism.[1] Monica and Teresa, like many of the re-spondents, also criticized other lesbian mothers who did not have the same philosophy. They embraced a politics of normality, which pro-moted restricted access to motherhood benefits for those who failed to attain their expectations about the ideal mother.

MONICA: I can't help that the kind of lesbian identity that the mothers have is also an issue as well. Because I do a lot of work on lesbian identity and I think that the farther out on the lesbian continuum, the mothers are from mainstream women, the more difficult it might become. I think if your mothers are really radical lesbian, it can be really tough. So, how mom looks when she comes to school is a big deal. Kids want you to be a garden-variety mom. So, if you have a mom who's way out there with a crew cut and pride chains and spiked hair and so for whatever orientation, that is going to be tough. And to add that in, I think it would be very difficult. So, I think the way the women, the way the couples present them-selves, is a big factor. I really do. Because I think the kids wanted us to be normal. Wanted us to appear normal. I think all kids want their parents to be normal. Normal as defined by the kids. The last thing that they want is to have to deal with if their mom is too fat or too whatever. I've had kids that didn't want their parents to come to school because their parents were too fat or too old or . . .

TERESA: . . . didn't speak English well. Or deaf.

MONICA: These are all issues. Our experiences have been pretty mainstream because *we're* so mainstream.

TERESA: Right. And it's been such a *normal* family.

MONICA: Just normal family, living out in rural America. Nothing re-ally traumatic. [. . .] And I think too, that as a parent, you have to *not* make it an issue. We never made it a big issue. We were never out there. I always thought it would be very difficult for the kids if I was on the news, like being this activist.

TERESA: And why? What was your father doing during Vietnam?

MONICA: Because my father was out there during Vietnam protest-ing—getting on the news, getting arrested, being an activist. And

I hated it! I hated it. It was so embarrassing to have this hippie father when everybody else's father wore a suit and was normal and so I didn't want to do that to them because I knew how hard that is to have that tension. Because parents are supposed to be all conservative and straightlaced. They are not supposed to be on the radical edge. So, it was important to me not to do that.

INTERVIEWER: So, you made a conscious decision not to do that?

MONICA: Yeah.

TERESA: And to make everything as regular and as easy as possible.

MONICA: Because we basically aren't very exotic. [laughing]

TERESA: Just sort of mom and dad! [laughing]

Woven into their narrative are ideologies that emanate from various discursive spheres including, motherhood, lesbian motherhood, and lesbian sexuality. Monica and Teresa strongly believed that they were successful parents, because they were able to dissociate their lesbianism from their motherhood to create and sustain outward appearances of normality. In the process, they relied heavily on molar ideologies of essential motherhood. By centralizing their similarities with other families, the couple's parenting strategies reinscribed dominant ideologies based on the heterosexual, patriarchal, nuclear family model. Their strategies aligned them with heterosexual mothers, but also created divisions among lesbian mothers. These divisions are similar to those depicted as "border work" in Barrie Thorne's (1995) study of school children. According to Thorne, interactions between groups can either reduce *or* reinforce differences. Monica's and Teresa's border work, concerning acceptable lesbian mothering, was divisive and perpetuated the oppressive ideologies that compelled them to separate their lesbianism from their motherhood in the first place. The ideologies played out through "border work" among the lesbian mothers have several key components. They portray motherhood/lesbianism and motherhood/nonmotherhood as oppositional dualisms, exaggerate differences between/among the groups, and downplay their commonalities. Through the construction of borders, the respondents reinscribe the essential motherhood ideologies described in the last chapter. However, at the same time, their strategies reveal the instability of these ideologies.

Becky and her partner, Lucille, adopted two young boys from Bulgaria and Guatemala. After a decade together, they were comfortable with one another and out about their lesbian relationship in all of their social networks. Becky's parents initially had a difficult time adjusting to their daughter's lesbianism, but the adoption of their sons had "helped people realize that we are just kind of like everybody else." Becky explained that she didn't think that lesbianism and motherhood had anything to do with each other. To emphasize her point, she said, "It's like, you can be a woman and a mom." Her comparison was interesting, because it contradicted the ideologies of essential motherhood, which unquestionably assume that motherhood and womanhood are one and the same experience. Becky indicated that one *could* be a woman and a mom, but this also suggested the possibility that these two experiences are not necessarily inseparable. Becky's statement, combined with her separation of her lesbianism and her mothering, simultaneously dismantled essential motherhood ideologies while also reifying them. Through Becky's denial of the connection between her lesbianism and her motherhood, she invoked the same molar ideologies of essential motherhood articulated by other respondents, such as Monica and Teresa. However, she also questioned the "natural" connection between woman and mother, thus deploying lines of flight that disrupted the seeming stable nature of those essential motherhood ideologies. Becky continued her narrative by once again drawing similarities between her experiences and other women who mother, regardless of their sexuality.

BECKY: For me, parenting was such a stress to adjust to that I would talk to people and say, "Tell me about this parenting thing." I was just a mom. I could listen to their horror stories, like one of my friends who locked herself in her room so that she could cry because she was having a hard time with her child because he was a little beast at the time. And those stories make me feel really good to think that people go through that I don't stop and say, "Gee. She's straight and I'm gay and we still feel the same way." We're all people.

Her partner, Lucille, agreed with Becky's assessment of the unimportance of their lesbianism to their mothering. Furthermore, she felt it was important to emphasize their similarity with other mothers in order to convey an image of acceptability and overcome people's misconceptions about lesbian motherhood.

LUCILLE: We know how important it is to let people know that there are positive experiences because I think when people—meaning heterosexual people—think about homosexuals, you just think of the negative stereotypes and you don't think of people like us and I think that's partly why we want to make sure that people know.

Lucille's narrative echoes the sentiments of other respondents who invoked a politics of normality to defend their right to parenthood. Lucille and Becky's defense of their mothering practices represents a reterritorialization of molar structures of motherhood. These women said that they thought that their families would be more accepted if they were more like other families. Because they recognized the cultural imperative to desexualize the maternal body, the respondents dismantled negative stereotypes about lesbian mothers by disengaging it from their mothering experiences. However, their stories about their everyday experiences highlight Gabb's (2001, p. 344) comment that she couldn't "leave my maternal status at the bedroom door, or my lesbian identity at the school gates: I *am* a lesbian/mother." The respondents' becomings are ongoing constellations of experiences that cling to the traditional ideals of motherhood while simultaneously instigating practices incompatible with motherhood ideologies that reveal their inherent instability. Subjectivity is a "betweenness" that emerges in the space between ideologies of lesbianism and motherhood. It is a trajectory of movements that can be envisioned as constant foldings and unfoldings of experiences that coagulate into lesbian motherhood bodies.

These examples are presented to illustrate my theoretical point: Personal narratives of lesbian motherhood are not just about similarity or assimilationism or reinscription of dominant ideologies. Rather, they are comprised of lines and flows that simultaneously reinforce molar ideologies through processes of reterritorialization, and reveal the instability of those ideologies through processes of deterritorialization. Hillary and Vicky's parenting story further exemplifies these processes.

DISCOURSES OF NORMALIZATION
AND THEIR INSTABILITIES

Hillary and Vicky were vivacious thirty-something mothers living in an upper-middle class suburb of Augustia where they both worked fulltime as medical professionals. Hillary, Vicky, and Nancy, their three-year-old daughter, greeted me at the door on the day of the interview. We took seats in the dining room, where we were surrounded by an array of boxes from their recent move into their newly built home. In addition to their excitement over their recent move, the couple also bubbled over with anticipation about the upcoming birth of their second child, conceived via artificial insemination from an unknown donor. Vicky's parents had traveled to Augustia to stay with them for several weeks in order to help them with the move and the upcoming birth of their grandchild. We could smell the delicious aromas drifting in from the kitchen where Vicky's mother prepared dinner while Vicky and Hillary talked with me in the dining room. Our close proximity to Vicky's mother later caused the couple to lower their voices to whispers as they discussed the difficulties they faced as they came-out to their families.

Hillary and Vicky's critique of the word "lesbian" was indicative of their philosophy about the unimportance of their sexuality compared to their mothering.

HILLARY: We really don't think of ourselves as/actually, to be honest with you, neither of us really care too much for that word, "lesbian." It really/to us, we're/

VICKY: . . . just moms.

HILLARY: Yeah—just moms. To us, it has been a word that has been kind of bastardized or stigmatized and/

VICKY: . . . labeled onto us but it's not who we are.

HILLARY: It's not how we would view ourselves. And actually, if someone would say/I think that we are actually more comfortable with being "gay" than being "lesbian." Which again, out there in the ranks of "you should be proud to be a lesbian." But neither one of us like that word so we're not going to say that word. We are comfortable with "partner" or "life partner." We are very comfortable

with that. And we are both real comfortable with being "life partners" and moms and/

VICKY: . . . raising a family.

HILLARY: So, "lesbian moms" doesn't ever, ever come up.

INTERVIEWER: How is "lesbian" different from being "gay"?

HILLARY: I never really knew that there was a difference but/

VICKY: . . . they are the same, I would think.

INTERVIEWER: But to the two of you, they are not the same.

HILLARY: They are not the same/they are the same to us, I guess, but it
seems to us that the culture has really made such a distinction between "gay" as men and "lesbian" as women and/

VICKY: And we are all just "gay." [. . .] Why do we need this title or
noun?

HILLARY: I would consider gay kind of an adjective. You have blond
hair, green eyes, and you are gay. As opposed to being "Lesbian."
And that's kind of/that's not really a word that I ever heard, really
until I came to Augustia.

Hillary and Vicky strongly delineated their own experiences from
those conventionally associated with lesbianism. Similar to Monica
and Teresa's critique of other lesbian mothers, Hillary and Vicky
erected a border between themselves and those lesbians who are stigmatized by mainstream society for their radical or unconventional
self-expression. In several places throughout their interview, Hillary
and Vicky described actions they took to be open and honest about
their lesbianism, while also distancing themselves from particular
ideologies about lesbianism that they saw as negative or contradictory to their understanding of what a good mother should be. Hillary
and Vicky expressed a desire to be accepted, yet only under certain
conditions that would emphasize specific aspects of their self-refer-
ence (i.e., mother) and de-emphasize others (i.e., radical lesbianism).
Paradoxically, however, the couple also repeatedly emphasized the
energy they spent disclosing their lesbianism to those in their social
networks.

For example, they explained how they had to "educate" their parents about lesbianism, when they first revealed their sexuality to them
many years ago. Their primary strategy during those educating inter-

actions emphasized how little their lesbianism changed their fundamental identities. Hillary described the tactics they took to slowly
introduce their parents to a new way of thinking about their daughters'
sexualities:

> I think the one thing that we both tried to do with both parents
> was to be very, very consistent. To say, "This is still me. I am
> still the same person. I haven't changed at *all*." [. . .] We tried to
> remain really consistent and calling even when it was really aw-
> ful and difficult to call. To still do it and still say, "This is still
> me. I haven't changed. This is still the way I live. These are still
> my hobbies. This is still what I do." So, it was hard. Very hard.

To clarify this point, I asked her if their parents thought that their
lesbianism had fundamentally altered their characters.

> Right—[they thought] that I was a changed person. So, that was
> tough. Very tough. Tough to see them struggling so hard with it.
> It was tough to remain patient when everything you see and ev-
> erything you read says that you had a lifetime to get used to it
> but they have only a weekend or whatever. So, patience and re-
> maining committed to that process was difficult. Very difficult.
> But over the course of the years, things have improved dramati-
> cally. But I think it is also a point, there's a point where they will
> go and then you have to recognize that/we actually struggle with
> even now to some extent is that we have to recognize that for
> parents, there's a point where their comfort level is and there's a
> point where they won't be comfortable. It's just a fact. They
> won't go beyond that point. And we just have to learn to accept
> that. And to respect that. And I think that is still something we
> struggle with: knowing where that point is.

This strategy of "educating" others about their lesbianism also
played a vital role in their commitment ceremony and their decision
to parent (a point I will return to later). Hillary and Vicky explained
how they spent several months prior to their commitment ceremony
disclosing their lesbianism to all those they were inviting so that they
would be comfortable. They clearly did not want to hide their lesbianism, yet they still declared that they are "just moms."

This kind of strategy, like Monica's and Teresa's gendered parenting practices described in the previous chapter, are often characterized as assimilationist, because they emphasize a certain part of identity that is understood to be more acceptable so that they can be part of the system rather than outside it. Yet, Hillary and Vicky stand with their feet firmly planted in their roles as mothers, while simultaneously re-alizing that the social location of "mother" can never fully capture their social experiences as lesbian mothers. This dual consciousness as lesbians and mothers illustrates the ways that their practices em-brace lines of flight that deterritorialize molar structures of family, woman, mother, and sexuality while simultaneously reterritorializing those same structures. They do not want to be "Lesbians" yet they recognize that their practices are characterized as lesbianism: they embrace lesbianism while also rejecting it.

. Intersection of lines and flows indicate a multiplicity to identity that goes far beyond conventional understandings of multiplicity where identities are composed of different parts that fit together into a whole. Instead, there is fluidity to Hillary and Vicky's accounts of self that show a lack of boundaries: they are forging identities that are always-already becoming something. Hillary and Vicky are the "other," while also they are not the "other." This process illustrates how otherness is within the system rather than outside it. Because they are both the same and the other, their becoming is a complex in-tersection of lines and flows of micropolitics that appear as molar representations of "lesbian mothers." Vicky and Hillary's embrace/ rejection of their otherness is a becoming, because it is an affirmation of the "positivity of difference"; a "multiple and constant process of transformation" (Braidotti, 1993, p. 44).

Similar to the way that I explained Monica and Teresa's experi-ences in Chapter 3, Hillary and Vicky's desire to be "just mothers" could be characterized as a political move stressing assimilationism. However, it is much more and highlights the inadequacy of conven-tional understandings of sexual identity that focus on the similarities and differences between homosexuality and heterosexuality. Further-more, Deleuze's conceptualization of "becoming" challenges any notion of politics that relies on an outside or an inside, resistance or assimilation. Instead, both processes flow together within the system simultaneously through the same strategies and practices of everyday life. This idea of a becoming doesn't imply that Hillary and Vicky are moving toward some state of being; rather, it is indicative of their perpetual constitution as social beings. They are at once lesbians, moms, both, and neither. The entire concept of "lesbian mom" dissolves under this scrutiny even though it continues to be a very real concept to them. Instead of "being," they are "becomings": they are not entities, subjects or things, but "a series of flows, energies, movements and capacities, a series of fragments or segments capable of being linked together in ways other than those that congeal [them] into an identity" (Grosz, 1994a, p. 198).

Other respondents' narratives also revealed the rhizomic linkages that constituted their becomings. In their stories about motherhood, respondents mapped their own multiplicities and illustrated their desire to avoid the dangers of micropolitics. With few exceptions (to be discussed in Chapter 7), the respondents felt insecure with the instability inherent in micropolitical flows. Consequently, they sought strategies that reinscribed molar categories. However, as Deleuze and Guattari (1987) point out, these molar categories are also inherently unstable and only serve as illusions of consistency, since they are omprised of the micropolitical flows associated with processes of deterritorialization. Hence, respondents pursued strategies of reterritorialization, but were faced with unavoidable flows associated with deterritorialization. In other words, reterritorialization was an attempt to demonstrate how similar their own experiences were to dominant ideologies of motherhood. These strategies, as I argued earlier in this chapter, concretize and reinforce essential motherhood ideologies. However, at the same time, their stories about their experiences indicate the multiple ways that their attempts to be "normal" are futile. This is not any reflection on the actual quality of their mothering practices; rather, it is indicative of the instability of these ideologies and the fractured nature of any attempts to perfectly embody them.

I met another respondent, Heather, in her small and sparsely furnished apartment in a small rural town between Augustia and Midland. The most noticeable feature of the small town was the abundance of large, elaborately built churches. Heather had recently returned to this small town, her hometown, after serving in the U.S. military. Her mother resided nearby and occasionally helped Heather care for her young son, who was conceived during her military service.

Heather was eagerly anticipating her girlfriend's upcoming move to live with her. They met online, spending many hours on the phone and several face-to-face meetings before they decided to cohabitate. Heather explained that she had denied her sexuality for a long time, because she feared that her coming-out might destroy her chances to become a mother. She explained that she had "*always* wanted children, [. . .] ever since she was little." While in her teens, she babysat many children and dreamed of having her own children. Her desire for children and her deeply Pentecostal religious roots kept her from acknowledging or accepting her own sexual desires: "Between religion and wanting to have kids. No—I'm going to be straight! I swear I am!" Heather had always thought that women must marry (or at least have some commitment to) men to have babies. Since her lesbianism would preclude her from marrying a man, she worried that she would never have a baby. Eventually, she decided that she could never fulfill the vision of motherhood defined by her religion and she set out to impregnate herself by having sex with servicemen she met in bars during her military service. She never knew the last names of these men and the only thing she knew for certainty about the identity of the baby's father was that he appeared to be African American. Heather described how emotionally grueling these seductions had been for her, because she had never been attracted to men and had never previously had sexual intercourse with a man.

Heather had embraced the mandates of essential motherhood, which dictated who could be a mother and under what circumstances. Heather spent much of her young adulthood struggling to decide whether she could ignore her sexual desire for other women in exchange for the fulfillment of her motherhood dreams. Her decision was further complicated by the deeply religious nature of family life in her childhood home. Homosexuality was strongly condemned. Heather explained how she struggled to find a way to embrace her religion, while still acknowledging her lesbianism. Her eventual decision to become pregnant as a single lesbian woman demonstrated an act of becoming whereby Heather's struggles with dominant ideologies about motherhood, religion, and sexuality were fractured to accommodate her unique desires. In Deleuze and Guattari terminology, her experiences of conception and motherhood as a single lesbian woman intersected those molar structures as a line of flight and disrupted their stability. Heather's story illustrates the incoherent multiplicities that make up a becoming; she could not simply add on elements of her identity and bring them together to form a stable sense of self. Instead, she simultaneously embraced the molar categories associated with essential motherhood, while also invoking strategies to become a mother that disrupted and intersected those molar categories.

Another respondent, Kim, had become a mother after foster parenting her two young nieces. Kim struggled with the intersection between her lesbianism and her new parental status, but her most central struggle revolved around the very notion that she could be a "legitimate mother," because she didn't follow the prescribed path to motherhood.

KIM: See, I don't feel like a legitimate mom. I'm not a part of the club. [Be]cause I never made that choice. You know. I never said, "I'm going to be a mom." [. . .] You know, "I'm going to go out and get pregnant or have sex" or . . . basically anything. That's what scary about it. [. . .] We actually decided *not* to have kids! Yeah. If it weren't for Alice and Mary, we wouldn't have that experience. [. . . I don't feel like a legitimate mother because . . .] I didn't go through the birthing process. I didn't even go through the/of course I might end up going through the foster care process. It's all goofed up. But, I didn't say, "Gee, I really want to have a kid." I didn't look through these photos and get interviewed and do home visits and choose the child I want. You know . . . do all that.

Kim had a clear notion of what it meant to be a "legitimate mother." Among the qualifications she perceived to be most important were giving birth to her child and/or finding one through the conventional, formalized routes offered by adoption agencies or insemination clinics. Kim did not follow any of those paths to motherhood, because she became foster mother for her nieces suddenly after her drug-addicted brother was no longer able to care for them. Consequently, she struggled over her own compatibility with molar ideologies about motherhood (i.e., "legitimate" avenues to motherhood).

Kim's perceptions about her mothering capacity were further complicated by the impact of her lesbianism on her legal guardianship status. Because she was very honest about her lesbianism to her family and the foster care system, she feared that their potential misconceptions about her sexuality might impair her ability to foster parent her nieces. Fortunately, she had not suffered any prejudices, but this did not preclude her from extensively worrying about it.

Kim's discomfort with her (self-defined) illegitimate motherhood status indicates one way that everyday experience can disrupt molar structures with lines of flight that contradict them. Kim's own mothering experiences belied essential motherhood ideologies. Her lesbianism further complicated her mothering experiences. However, amidst these contradictions, she held firmly to the ideologies and defined her own experiences as indications of deficiency (hence, her status as an "illegitimate mother"). When I spoke to Kim a few months later, I found that she had embraced her status as mother and no longer felt compelled to question her legitimacy. Her eventual embrace of the molar structures surrounding motherhood reveals the constant reterritorialization that always accompanies micropolitical processes.

Sophia, like other respondents, claimed that lesbianism had little to do with her mothering.

SOPHIA: I don't really think about myself as a lesbian. I just think of myself as a mom. As far as a mom, I don't think of myself as a lesbian. I mean, that doesn't enter into it, I don't think. I don't think that has anything to do with it.

Sophia had spent the majority of her children's lives in a heterosexual marriage, with little thought about her own sexual orientation. Her realization about her lesbianism was a slow process that finally crested about fifteen years into her marriage. She came-out to her husband, who was initially supportive, but later became angry and vindictive. Sophia's life changed dramatically when her husband refused to continue divorce mediation and went to court to gain custody of their children. Sophia was financially insecure after spending her entire married life as a stay-at-home mother. She couldn't afford a lawyer and was forced to use a public defender, who was inexperienced and ignorant about gay issues. Tragically, Sophia lost custody of her children.

SOPHIA: He won and I lost custody, because I was a lesbian. They said in the papers that it had nothing to do with the fact that I was a lesbian, but the whole custody trial centered on what I was doing as a lesbian: what books I was reading, who I was seeing, what kinds of meetings I was going to. There was not one question about my mothering or my mothering ability. That was all thrown out the window.

Her post-divorce life was extremely difficult as she tried to financially support herself on part-time jobs and attend classes to get a degree. She saw little of her children because her husband dictated visitation. Furthermore, her teenage children didn't like visiting her because her apartment was too cramped. Sophia kept her lesbianism secret from her children, until she decided to come-out to her daughter. She had not revealed her sexual orientation to her son at the time of interview because she feared he would react negatively. At the end of the interview, she rhetorically raised the question, "Has [my lesbianism] affected the way that I raised my kids?"

Maybe, I don't know. I guess I really didn't know how to raise a daughter, like primping with the hair and makeup. [. . .] I guess I grew up thinking that it did. I was thinking that something was wrong with me because I wasn't feminine. I think it was easier to deal with boys. [. . .] I think I felt more comfortable with that. My daughter is very feminine. She wears makeup and finger nail polish and a whole pile of crap. [laughing] She always plants these lipstick kisses on the side of my face or on my coffee cup or whatever and I say, "Why do you wear all that stuff?" She laughs.

Similar to Kim, who also felt that she didn't "fit" proper expectations about mothering, Sophia said that her own style of parenting had always been subtly shaped by her own feelings of difference from other women. She felt that she often lacked the traditional feminine connections that mothers are expected to have with their daughters. Thus, her sexuality did not explicitly connect with her mothering, but yet it did. Sophia was uncomfortable with the ideologies that accompany gendered interactions with children, and thus felt more comfortable interacting with her sons than with her daughter. Her narrative indicates her uncertainty over the influence that her sexuality may or may not have on her mothering. The connection between lesbianism and mothering is something that she has been acculturated to deemphasize. However, upon introspection, she describes ways that it may have had a subtle impact on her interactions with her children. Her story indicates how she was drawn to the seeming stability of the molar structures that make up essential motherhood, yet her own experiences never really fit those expectations, thus indicating the fractured micropolitical lines that deterritorialized those structures. Sophia's response was interesting, because she simultaneously invoked the molar ideologies associated with motherhood and also the lines of flight that intersect those ideologies. She reinscribed the essential motherhood mandate that dictates the separation of motherhood from sexuality, especially lesbian sexuality. However, she then acknowledged that her practices of motherhood have always been disrupted by her inability to conform to the expectations that surround the mothering of her daughter. The differences between Sophia's daughter's articulations of femininity and her own definitions of femininity made her to question her earlier assumption about the dissociation between her sexuality and her motherhood. Thus, she wondered whether her lesbianism was what made her unable to act feminine in a socially prescribed fashion. At the same time, however, processes of reterritorialization underscored her questioning: she equated her inability to master certain hegemonic practices of femininity with lesbianism. This line of reasoning led her back to molar structures about lesbian sexuality that assume womanhood and femininity are not compatible in the absence of heterosexuality. Her experience of self as a lesbian mother, consequently, was comprised of a multiplicity of movements and instabilities that constituted her becoming.

Sophie's narrative, like some of the respondents previously described, is much more complex than it first appears, thus underscoring the processes that make up a practice of "becoming." These becomings illustrate Deleuze and Guattari's conceptualization of individuals as vast collections of movements rather than unified entities. The respondents' perceptions about their lesbian motherhood experiences resoundingly deconstructed the notion of a "lesbian mother" entity. Their experiences indicated the movements, flows, contradictions, and multiplicities that make up experience. Those seemingly contradictory experiences constituted their becomings.

BECOMING A MOTHER

The mothering status of the forty respondents in this study represented a variety of different biological and legal connections between child and parent. Some respondents were the biological, gestational mother to their children. The connections between these women and their children were experienced unquestionably and rarely examined by the respondents. Other women held varying legal and biological connections to their children. These women included adoptive mothers, stepmothers, comothers, and foster mothers. The experiences of lesbian mothers are interesting, because they simultaneously reinscribe conventional ideologies about maternal connections between mothers and children while also challenging them through the creation of maternal connections between nonbiological mothers and their children. As Jennifer Harding (1998, p. 110) points out, motherhood practices most often work to confirm heterosexuality and biological connections between children, mothers, and father.

> Motherhood, as a practice of femininity, is persistently produced through various discourses, spoken from different institutional sites, as a way of understanding the materiality of the body which underpins and confirms hetero-sex/uality and grounds it in biology. Biological discourse produces maternity as a process which includes all women (potentially and actually) in a seamless category of sameness.

However, all mothers are not alike, and their lived experiences are shaped by socioeconomic status, race and ethnicity, disability, age, and sexual orientation. These differing experiences produce varying articulations of motherhood that contradict conventional ideologies.

> Our understandings of motherhood are formed through representations which indicate "what constitutes good or bad mothering" and, even, those "for whom motherhood is or is not appropriate" But maternity might be achieved through various different routes (sexual intercourse, artificial insemination, *in vitro* fertilization, adoption or step-parenting) and might intersect with other subject positions. (Harding, 1998, p. 110)

Lesbian mothers pose an interesting case study, because they illustrate great variability through their parenting stories. Their narratives reinscribe conventional molar structures of motherhood, while also revealing the instability of these various subject positions. Inconsistencies become particularly visible in discussions about AI families and blended families, where questions about biological and legal connections between parents and children are experienced most acutely.

Respondents with families created using AI or through blended arrangements often strategically situated themselves in relation to various molar categories, in order to defend their decision, particularly to their families-of-origin. For these respondents, molar structures represented safety and security. Ideologies of motherhood, genetics, and gender relations provided convincing reasons for validating their parenting decisions. However, these ideologies were also restrictive. They failed to capture the unique aspects of lesbian mothering experiences, thus requiring mothers to defend themselves against ideologies that rebuked their legitimacy. Their own experiences never neatly fit into these molar structures; respondents were always-already representing lines of flight that disrupted the stability of those molar structures. Most of the respondents struggled with their inability to conform to essential motherhood ideologies, and they feared instability and the lines of flight that accompanied processes of deterritorialization. As the following examples will illustrate, they were unable to reterritorialize and neatly coalesce their own experiences with dominant ideologies of motherhood despite their best efforts.

Wilma mothered two daughters, ages nineteen and twenty-four, who were born during Wilma's previous marriage to the girls' father. She and her partner, Samantha, had been living together with Wilma's children for several years. Wilma described Samantha's integration into their newly created blended family as very difficult. Wilma's teenage daughters resisted Samantha's enthusiastic attempts to become their stepmother. Like respondents described previously, Wilma's defense of her lesbian parenting relied heavily on asserting the normality of her family's experiences. She critiqued lesbian parenting strategies, in general, to characterize some mothering strategies as productive and others as counterproductive. Interestingly, her defense of a normalizing strategy implied that she recognized that there was something different about lesbian families.

WILMA: Depending on the way the child was conceived—"got," we'll call it—they might have the real father be involved. And as long as there's that "this-is-normal" attitude, the "this-is-okay" attitude, the "there's nothing wrong with what we're doing" attitude, then the child will grow up to be a normal, well-balanced child and there's nothing to say that that child will be homosexual. I was raised by heterosexual parents and you know what, we are not all pedophiles! [chuckling]

Wilma situated herself squarely in the appropriate motherhood tier of DiLapi's hierarchy, while legitimating lesbian mothering. Once again, this suggests that lesbian mothers themselves are implicated in the construction and deployment of discourses and practices that valorize the ideals epitomized by the ideal mother. Although many outsiders view lesbian motherhood as oxymoronic, lesbian women themselves live within the same social world and thus experience the same powerful pronatalistic messages. They also work to reinscribe those ideologies. The maternal mystique demands that women conceive children: "Ultimate fulfillment *as a woman* is achieved by becoming a mother" (Hoffnung, 1998, p. 282). For lesbian women, the decision to bear children outside a heterosexual relationship presents certain challenges. Several of the respondents in this study discussed their inability to conceive after seeking artificial insemination.

Becky and Lucille were the adoptive parents of two young international boys (from Guatemala and Bulgaria, as described in Chapter 5). The adoption of their sons occurred after several years of agonizing attempts by Lucille to become pregnant. Adoption was eventually chosen as their route to motherhood because Becky had no desire to conceive a child. In fact, Becky was not even sure she wanted to be a mother when the couple first began the insemination process. She continued to express reservations about parenthood even after several years of unsuccessful attempts to inseminate Lucille and their resulting decision to pursue international adoption.

LUCILLE: She wasn't ready for them and I had to wait for her to be ready for them. But then we had to pay those bills to go get inseminated and those were not small bills.

BECKY: Yeah, I wasn't as disappointed as her when she didn't get pregnant. [. . .] The first year, I was pretty relieved. The second year, I was kind of like "Well, that's kind of too bad it didn't work." I was kind of building up to it. [. . .] Being a parent is a big stretch for me. Lucille always wanted to be a parent. I thought it might be a nice thing to do someday, but I'm not sure that "someday" would have ever come. I guess I couldn't see myself as an adult for a while. That whole responsibility of being responsible for somebody else. When we got [our oldest son] in Bulgaria on probably the fourth night or so and he had had a really bad day and he just cried and cried and cried. We don't know why, but we sent him to stay with the sitter. Lucille said, "Do you want to stay with him or do you want him to go with a sitter?" and I said, "Please send him to the sitter." And he was fine. She could speak Bulgarian which helped and/

LUCILLE: She was a grandmotherly figure and very warm with him and . . .

BECKY: And I think we were trying to wait on him which was completely foreign. In addition to not speaking the language and he was probably so confused. He just cried and cried and nothing we did helped and I was just terrified and thought "What have I done!" All I could envision was him as a teenager being drunk. Things that all parents probably go through, but they have their relationship already in place and I was just sort of feeling isolated like "What am I doing? I don't know how to do this!"

LUCILLE: Just the same as any other parent, though. Because I can remember I was talking to her and she said, "I don't think I can do this." It's a little late now, don't you think? But her good friend we had spoken with and she had had a baby right around the time that we went to get [our oldest son] and [our friend] said that she and her husband had the same conversation: they were ready to give birth and a few days prior to the birth, they said/

BECKY: "We changed our minds! We aren't doing this!" [laughing]

LUCILLE: So, I said, "Honey, it's normal." It just happens. You get scared.

Becky and Lucille portrayed Becky's uncertainty as "normal" and accentuated her similarities to their heterosexual friends and their stories about parenting uncertainties. Within the maternal mystique, such uncertainty is acceptable and even anticipated and should not be perceived as a reason for giving up the desire to parent. The couple's understanding of Becky's uncertainty emphasized their similarity to other prospective parents, while also underscoring the differences that exist between them. Because womanhood is equated with motherhood in our culture and lesbianism is disassociated with both motherhood and womanhood, lesbian mothers have a vested interest in dismantling these divisions. However, their strategies often fail to dismantle these binary divisions; instead, they work to stretch them to include lesbian mothers. Consequently, other articulations of womanhood and lesbianism are further marginalized.

Becky and Lucille's characterization of the "normality" of their experiences also glossed over aspects of their adoption experience that were not typical. For example, they spent many weeks in Bulgaria, as they visited countless orphanages in an attempt to find an available child. During that experience, they never dared openly acknowledge that they were a couple. Furthermore, only Lucille was able to legally adopt their Bulgarian son. They explained that their inability to immediately jointly adopt was due to the fact that they were unmarried, which was ultimately due to their lesbianism. Only later, upon returning to the United States, could Becky initiate second-parent adoption procedures.

The contradictions inherent in the respondents' parenting strategies were revealed particularly well among those couples who chose to conceive through artificial inseminate. Tania and Paula explained how Tania had really wanted to give birth to a child for them until she experienced medical problems requiring a hysterectomy. It took some time for her to recover emotionally from that experience, at which time they decided that they would try foster parenting in order to see "how we would work together as parents." They became the first gay or lesbian foster parents in their suburban county. After foster parenting a nine-year-old girl with severe emotional problems, they decided to give birth to their own children. Paula's decision to become pregnant was a radical shift from her earlier reticence to have children. She had never wanted to experience pregnancy, and in fact, had initially resisted pursuing AI when Tania had tried to become pregnant before her hysterectomy. Paula quickly became pregnant with the help of a local AI clinic, giving birth to two daughters.

PAULA: We were lying in bed one night and I said, "I think we should have children." And Tania said, "Yeah. Right." And I said, "No. I'm going to call the doctor tomorrow." And she said, "Yeah. Right. [sarcastically]"

TANIA: At this point, I was the furthest I had ever been away from having kids that I had been in my whole life. With the hysterectomy, dealing with that and then thinking that that part of me is done and over and we already did the roller-coaster ride with her and then she pops off and says this. I said, "No, I don't want to have a kid." She said, "Let's do it." I said, "No, I don't want to."

PAULA: But I think probably heterosexual couples go through it too but they don't have/it's almost expected of them so they just go along with it and if they actually thought about it, that they have a choice, then they would have the same conversations.

Tania and Paula's pathway to parenthood illustrates the strength of essential motherhood ideologies on several levels. Tania described how her hysterectomy radically undermined her own feelings of femininity, because she had always equated womanhood with motherhood. Both women eventually came to feel that their lives were incomplete without children, consequently, seeking foster parent status and AI services to attain those goals. However, along the way, both experienced trepidation about parenting. Like Lucille and Becky, they interpreted their nervousness as a "normal" symptom experienced by anyone that considers parenthood.

> I think probably heterosexual couples go through it too, but [childbearing] is always expected of them so they just go along with it and if they actually thought about it—that they had a choice—then they would have the same conversation.

However, the couple clearly recognized that their experiences differed from heterosexual parents because they had to take premeditated steps to achieve parenthood. The extra steps required by lesbian couples to achieve parenthood sometimes impeded women's desires to become parents. Paula and Tania explained that their initial attempts to foster parent were stymied by parents who did not want their children to be placed in a foster home with a lesbian couple.

Patriarchal notions of family life also structure adoptions. For example, most international adoptions require a couple to be legally married in order for them to both legally adopt the children. Since lesbian women cannot legally marry, this requirement forces one of them to remain legally invisible to the child until they can attain second-parent adoption in the United States. And this is not a certainty since only a limited number of states allow second-parent adoptions for lesbian women. Becky and Lucille strategically negotiated the complicated process of internationally adopting their children. In their first inquiries, they were informed that it was not possible for them to adopt their children as a couple, because they were not married. Therefore, they decided that Lucille would initially become the legal adoptive parent for their sons. This left Becky without any legal recognition for over a year after they adopted their first son. Although they planned to eventually pursue second-parent adoption to legalize Becky's ties to their children, they realized that they had to wait until both boys had been adopted first by Lucille. They were compelled to wait until Lucille had adopted both boys, because they feared that the home study resulting from his second-adoption might spoil their chances of another international adoption by a country that discriminates against lesbian couples. Lucille explained,

> We wanted to wait and adopt them both at the same time because we/if we had both adopted our oldest son prior to adopting our youngest son, then that would have had to go on the home study and you don't know what that would have put in the foreign country's mind. Because you have to put both adoptive parent's names down.

They also explained that they had wanted to adopt two boys from the same country but Bulgaria [the country from which they adopted their oldest/first son] would not allow a single woman to adopt more than one child. Since they could not marry, they were forced to seek a child in another country.

Other respondents in the study described roadblocks to achieving motherhood via AI. Heidi, for example, doubted that she and her partner would pursue insemination through a clinic, because they could not afford the high cost of the procedure. Tyler, the mother of a young daughter conceived during a previous relationship with a man, explained that she would never use a clinic for insemination, because she didn't want her pregnancy to be structured by the medical establishment. She explained:

TYLER: But I didn't want something so simple as having a baby to either be in the hands of a doctor, in terms of going through a doctor for artificial insemination. I just don't think it has anything to do with medicine. It's not a medical procedure. You know? I think that's a violation. That just doing something so simple requires a doctor. I just think that is an insult to my intelligence. Not to my body, but to my intelligence. The basic reproduction is not that difficult [chuckle].

Even when couples had the resources and desire to pursue AI, they faced persistent societal reluctance to willingly grant lesbian couples unencumbered access to insemination and adoption resources. Not all clinics are willing to inseminate lesbian women. Those clinics that do provide services to lesbians often lack sensitivity to the unique needs of their lesbian clients. For example, the AI clinic director commented to Becky and Lucille, "It amazes me that lesbian couples have been so positive coming in here. It's really quite a change." Becky recognized that the director was defining their pursuit of AI through his own preconceived notions of insemination by heterosexual couples.

> She had no connection that for us, it was the only option of having children. And the heterosexual couples coming in, they are there because they have already had a failure and this is just a reminder of that failure. For us, there was no failure. We couldn't do anything to have kids otherwise. I was really surprised that she didn't put that together.

Becky's observation reflected the lack of sensitivity to lesbian clients' needs and also highlighted my earlier point about the difference between heterosexual couples' decision to parent and a lesbian couples' decision to parent: heterosexual couples can become pregnant, whether or not a decision has been made to do so, while lesbian women must actively take steps to become pregnant.

A lesbian couple's need to plan and actively seek out insemination services (whether it is through a clinic, self-insemination, or through sexual intercourse with a man) is sometimes characterized as "free agency." Jenny Wald (1997) argues that lesbians choosing to parent pose a direct challenge to the patriarchal foundation of hegemonic ideologies about what sorts of relationships constitute a family. Lesbian parenting challenges the definition of female reproduction as natural and undermines the foundations of patriarchy by deleting the male role and making childbearing a choice by and for women (Wald, 1997).

AI or adoptive lesbian couples pose the clearest challenge to hegemonic ideologies of family. However, parenting is not just a single act of insemination; rather, it is a whole constellation of discourses and practices that come together to form an ideology of parenthood. Consequently, what might initially be characterized as an act of subversion is quickly reterritorialized through other everyday parenting practices that perpetuate the very ideologies that their micropolitical strategies initially invoked. Hillary and Vicky's experiences "educating" their parents about their plans to parent illustrated the complexity of becoming processes and the interlocking nature of micro and macropolitical processes.

Hillary and Vicky, who were introduced earlier in this chapter, were pregnant with their second child when I met them. They described how they were forced to "educate" their parents when they decided to form a family via artificial insemination. Vicky's parents expressed reservations about the insemination process as well as fears that their grandchild would lack a father figure.

VICKY: Because they were very comfortable with us as a couple but then when we said that we were going to have kids, they back-slid.

HILLARY: Big time!

VICKY: Yeah—so it was like we had to totally reeducate all over again. And then they struggled with the issues of their father. Would they be missing out on a father figure?

HILLARY: When both of our fathers are so important to us as such a mainstay and a role for us, how could we possibly do that!?

VICKY: "What will you tell this child?" So, we had to reeducate our families about artificial insemination and how does the process happen and how are going to raise/what are we going to tell the kids when they are older and they look for who is their dad. "Who am I like?" And all that genetic type issues. [. . .] We worked *much* harder! Then we would compare to times like when her brother was having a child and they didn't get any hassle. And here we get a litany of questions and concerns and they were really against it.

Later in the interview, the couple explained how Hillary's parents also expressed concerns about their plans to have children. However, Hillary's parents' concerns were somewhat different than those expressed by Vicky's parents. Hillary's parents feared that they wouldn't feel like grandparents, because they lacked biological and legal connection to their grandchildren.

HILLARY: My parents struggled significantly with children. [. . .] I think that they thought they couldn't really be considered grandparents because it had nothing to do with me.

VICKY: Boy, they really struggled with that.

HILLARY: Very much. "Will they call us grandma?" and all that.

VICKY: And they actually chose not to be called that. They came up with names that they wanted to/

HILLARY: "Nanna" and "Gramps." They just didn't feel/

VICKY: So, we just respected that.

INTERVIEWER: At that point, were you considering second-parent adoption?

HILLARY: Yes.

INTERVIEWER: At that point, did they know that?

HILLARY: Oh, yeah. But again, through the whole process we certainly knew that that was definitely an option.

INTERVIEWER: But didn't your parents see that as a legitimating/

HILLARY: Oh, no. Still no connection.

VICKY: Still no connection.

INTERVIEWER: It had to be a blood connection?

HILLARY: Yeah. And then it was this thing about the father. My dad struggled with that a lot. An awful lot.

VICKY: I think he still struggles with that.

HILLARY: Yeah, I would say.

INTERVIEWER: How do you respond to that?

HILLARY: Oh, boy. "Why would you want children?" and I said, "Did anyone ever ask you why you would want children? What would your answer be if someone had asked you before you had had me? I'm your first born so what would you have said? Why did *you* want children?"

VICKY: We put it back on them.

HILLARY: "Any sort of answer that you would have would also be our answer as well." And, I think that my mom went through this period where she felt that it was very selfish. Very selfish to do that to a child. To a child. "You are just doing it to meet your own needs. It's very selfish of you to bring a child into that environment or realm." And the thing that we *did* struggle with on both ends was difficult was this father issue and the issue of how do you present that to your dads who are very important to you and whose relationship you cherish? [. . .] It's a hard thing to get across. But, the reality was that we kept going with it because this is our only option.

In addition to their worries about the affect on the child, Hillary's and Vicky's parents also worried about how others would react to their grandparenthood. Children increase the likelihood of comments from outside the family. Grandparents may be exposed to questions that they don't feel comfortable addressing. Grandparents also may be concerned that their grandchildren will have difficulties coping with people who do not understand their family arrangement. Hillary's parents encouraged the couple to adopt a child rather than have their own children via artificial insemination for that reason.

VICKY: [They wanted us to adopt] because we could be saving some child out there from some horrible life. So why not adopt? But I was like, I've always wanted to have kids! If we can have kids, then let's have our own. I think in their mind, it made it easier to accept: "Oh, they adopted a baby because it was in some little foreign country and it was malnourished or whatever." And it would be easier to tell people. "How will I present that?" And you could see it when we would go home their hesitation introducing me and then here's this baby. "Is this Hillary's daughter or not?" You know what I mean?

Hillary's parents' discomfort was particularly evident when they accompanied their daughters and grandchildren into the public domain where they were forced to verbally acknowledge their daughter's alternative family.

VICKY: They would struggle like when we would go out to restaurants and her parents would see friends that they know, saying, "Here's my daughter." And then you would hear the hesitation, so we would just let them go with whatever they felt.

HILLARY: But they are much better with it now: "This is Hillary and this is Vicky, her partner, and this is their daughter." So they have gotten much better with it.

VICKY: It has taken a while.

INTERVIEWER: So now they think of themselves as grandparents?

VICKY & HILLARY [together]: Yeah, I think so.

VICKY: I mean, when she calls them "Gramps & Nana, where are you?" I think that does it. But then again, they wanted to know why we were having another one. So, then we had to struggle with that all over again. We did.

Hillary and Vicky were sympathetic to their parents' discomfort, but were also frustrated, because they did not feel comfortable with their parents' desire to conceal the nature of their family relationships. This frustration resurfaced when Hillary and Vicky baptized their children.

VICKY: And that was an educational process, again. My folks were like, "You mean two women are going to stand up there?" I was like, "Well, yeah, she is the other parent!" But, "What will people think? You have to have a man up there!" So, my mother wanted my brother to be my "husband." So, we stood up and said, "No." So it was like this whole, "What will people think?"

HILLARY: That drives an awful lot of everything.

VICKY: For my side.

HILLARY: Which is a big factor. You struggle between creating our own identity and then also being respectful to find some sort of/

VICKY: I'm not out [in my hometown]. They prefer me not to be. [...] They do not want to be out to anybody.

HILLARY: They don't want to be out to anybody. It's very different [from my parents].

VICKY: I said, "What do you think is going to happen when [our daughter] comes and calls [Hillary] 'momma'?"

HILLARY: But the reality is that most of her aunts and uncles and cousins know and they are fine. Back before our ceremony, they wanted us to take our rings off.

VICKY: Yeah, they wanted us to take our rings off and I thought about it and I thought, "No! I'm not taking my ring off. Because what does that say"/

HILLARY: . . . about us!? And when we get a child, we are not going to do this. So that was a real education. "No, we are not going to do this."

Vicky and Hillary felt pressured by their parents to pretend that they were not lesbian coparents when they were introduced to one of their parents' friends or acquaintances.

VICKY: So, initially, I find myself calling her "Hillary" when talking to [our daughter]. Because, depending on where we were. Because it was so easy to say, "Go see mom." But we finally quit that because you can't send mixed messages to a child without making the child feel bad. "Why is it okay here but not there?" And we are very comfortable here. No problem. We are out to everyone and it doesn't matter. Just don't bring it home! It's a very small town. [. . .] So, little by little we just try to educate people.

Hillary and Vicky's strategy of "educating" others about their family was only effective if they believed that their own experiences somehow coincided with "acceptable" or conventional ideologies about motherhood. The underlying purpose of their education strategies was to demonstrate to others their normality and similarity to other parents. Hillary, for example, said she "turned the tables" back on her father when he asked why they thought they should become parents. Furthermore, Hillary and Vicky's emphasis on similarity through educating strategies required that they conceal any differences from others as well as concealing those differences from themselves. Their reluctance to recognize the instability of the very ideologies they sought to attain was common among the respondents. They sought to compartmentalize their identities so that their mothering and their sexuality would never overlap; however, at the same time, they were constantly reminded of the impossibility of that task. Their parents also faced a similar quandary, but of a different quality: they recognized that their daughters failed to conform to dominant ideologies of motherhood, but instead of attempting to squeeze them into those categories, they dismissed their daughters' potential to mother. The result was a veritable tug-of-war in which neither side won but both sides instigated molar lines and molecular lines that disrupted and undermined molar unities of motherhood and family.

This interaction between Hillary, Vicky, and their parents illustrated the interconnected nature of becomings—none exist as independent entities but only as circulations and flows that overlap and play off each other in rhizomic fashion. The process of becoming is never an isolated event; it occurs in our bedrooms, living rooms and communities. Bodies are contained within flesh but subjectivities exist as systems of flows and intensities that are constantly invoked. The networks of interrelations resulting from social interactions form rhizomic interconnections that simultaneously feed micro and macropolitical processes. Hillary, Vicky, and their parents struggled with the fact that lesbian motherhood is a process of becoming where the slippages associated with molecular lines of flight are quite distinct. However, at the same time, their practices disguised micropolitical flows and their workings of power through the constant reinscription of molar ideologies associated with family and motherhood. Lesbian mothers, like Hillary and Vicky, were caught in a maelstrom of limitations and opportunities. Because of the strength of molar lines, many lesbian moms avoid the risks associated with radical displays of their sexuality. However, in the midst of everyday interactions, their strategies revealed that their experiences were always-already radical because, by definition, their experiences of motherhood disrupted the molar categories that they attempted to embrace.

Chapter 6

Coming-Out

In the previous chapters, I explored the ways that micro- and macropolitical lines and flows are simultaneously deployed within the respondents' narratives of motherhood. The respondents' stories indicated that they disengaged their sexuality from their parenting. However, their stories also revealed their inevitable inability to create seamless stories of normality, because their experiences were complexly dislocated by micropolitical movements. In this chapter, I examine these same processes through the mothers' stories about their sexual awakenings and its impact on their parenting.

Paula Rust's (1993) work suggested that individuals in everyday social interactions rarely recognize the instability of their own identities. Hillary and Vicky's experiences indicated a conscious effort to overcome instability and present a consistent image of self to others around them. However, as I've pointed out throughout this book, consistency is merely a mirage that is underscored by a multiplicity of identity sites through which power works to oppress, control, and dominate. In the following section, I will examine the strategies Hillary and Vicky used to forge a consistent sense of self. Then, I will carefully locate those strategies within a more complex framework of lines and flows that are revealed through the cracks and fissures that underscored their narratives. It is the combination of these flows of deterritorialization and lines of reterritorialization that constituted their subjectivities. Their example is extended to other respondents' stories about their sexual identities.

Lesbian Motherhood: Stories of Becoming
© 2007 by The Haworth Press, Inc. All rights reserved.
doi:10.1300/5922_07

HILLARY AND VICKY:
DISRUPTING CATEGORIES

As you will recall from previous chapters, Hillary and Vicky had been together for over ten years. They met during college before either of them had acknowledged their lesbian desire. They forged a close bond during their undergraduate years that persevered through a long-distance separation and Vicky's first lesbian live-in lover. During the early years of their friendship, they both sensed something deeper beneath their friendship, but neither felt inclined to acknowledge it. In fact, Vicky said she resisted her sexual attraction to women, because she feared that it would prohibit her from becoming a mother: "I think I was going through the denial thing because I was going to get married because I had to be married to have kids. That whole bit."

Hillary and Vicky attributed their initial attraction to the similarities in their upbringings. Both women came from what they described as "stable," "religious" families. Their shared backgrounds and a desire for family swiftly became the predominant theme underlying the couple's narratives. Vicky explained that she didn't expect her first lesbian relationship to last: "I met somebody and we had a place together. But it still wasn't what I wanted. I still wanted a family, but never thought it would ever happen." Hillary describes her discovery of a gay-supportive religious organization as "the turning point" in their search for the kind of life they had both envisioned. Although Hillary had accepted her lesbianism, she had not disclosed it to anyone else. Furthermore, she didn't have time to pursue any social activities in which she could meet other gays and lesbians due to the rigorous demands of her medical residency program. Therefore, her decision to attend a Dignity and Integrity meeting was one made with great nervousness and trepidation. With humor, she remembered calling the facilitator several times until the woman finally said, "Are you coming or not? You seem real hesitant. This is like the fifth phone call. I can't really tell you any more about it. You just need to come. Are you coming or not?" Although Vicky and Hillary were living in different states at the time, Hillary sought Vicky's support in her decision to attend the meeting, because she sensed that it possibly held the key to their dreams of becoming a family. "I kept telling

Vicky that I'm convinced that it is out there, I just don't know where."
When I asked her to clarify what she meant by "it," she replied,

HILLARY: "It" being a [. . .] lifestyle where you could live together and
be a family and not be considered something unusual. Not someone like those people marching in the parades, carrying the ban-
ners and waving the flags and being, you know, *not* what we were.
There had to be someplace where you could still be normal. And I
kept convincing myself that it was somewhere.

When Hillary finally found the courage to attend her first Dignity
and Integrity meeting, she was pleasantly surprised to find that the
members fulfilled her hopes and expectations about what it meant to
be gay. Hillary and Vicky believed that their lesbianism was not
something that they wanted to call attention to; rather, they desired
access to the rights and privileges afforded other couples wanting to
form a family. As women who valued their similarities to other heterosexual mothers, they felt disconnected and judgmental about other
gays and lesbians who were more radical about their sexual identities. Hillary was pleased to find that Augustia's Dignity and Integrity
group was comprised of a "normal" group of men and women. They
maintained close friendships with many of the members a decade after joining the group.

HILLARY: But I was terrified [when I attended the first meeting of
Dignity and Integrity]! I told Vicky that the doors of the church
never felt so heavy! [laughing] That night trying to open it. But it
turned out to be this really neat circle of friends. Very warm, very
accepting. And it wasn't cultish. It was a traditional religious service like I had always been exposed to. It felt very comfortable.
The people were normal. These were professional people that did
day-to-day things and felt just like me and nobody wore funky
clothes [. . .]. Everything was fine. I felt very comfortable. People
made me feel very welcome. So at that point, my circle of friends
was definitely starting to circle around Dignity and Integrity. Even
to this day, twelve or thirteen years later.[1]

Shortly after Hillary attended the Dignity and Integrity meeting,
Vicky visited Hillary and decided to move to Augustia. She found a
job, and they maintained separate residences for over a year as they

reacquainted themselves with each other after living apart for several years. Eventually, the couple's regular involvement with Dignity and Integrity became the impetus for Hillary to come-out to her parents.

Hillary and Vicky's "comfort" with the "normality" of those in Dignity and Integrity was equaled by the couple's discomfort with certain articulations of lesbian identity. In fact, the very term "lesbian" made them uncomfortable, because they believed it signified an identity that did not fit with their daily lives as lesbian mothers. At the end of this chapter I present a narrative excerpt that reveals the subtle integration of micropolitics and macropolitics within the couple's critique of the label, "lesbian." However, before doing so, I provide the background that leads to their critique. It is only through the embrace of stability that many of the respondents in this study were able to disguise the lines of flight in their own narratives. The following sections, which lead up to Hillary and Vicky's critique of "lesbian" at the end of this chapter, illustrate the strategies employed by the respondents as they embraced processes of reterritorialization. Perhaps most interesting are those instances where the deterritorialization that always accompanies that reterritorialization is revealed.

DIFFERENCE + BIOLOGY (MUST) = LESBIANISM

Hillary's parents' were not supportive when Hillary revealed her lesbianism to them. However, her father slowly accepted it and encouraged Hillary's mother to do the same. Hillary's father based his acceptance on the belief that homosexuality is a biological attribute that is given to people by God.

HILLARY: So [the tension with my parents over my coming-out] was awkward and strained and that took a long time to get over. It's interesting because my mom is a teacher so she's the reader of the family and my dad is the one that reads a few choice magazines and the newspaper and that was the extent of his leisure reading. And here's my dad literally walking around the house reading my mom this material trying to [educate her]. My dad was *much* better than my mom was. So, I encouraged my dad to think of it this way: "If this is something I've always been and not just a decision that I have made, then why would I *choose* to be this? *I* wouldn't choose this. But I'm comfortable with this. This is *me*." And I always told them that I credited them with the reason that I *am* so comfortable with it. It's because I had great self-esteem and it was how I was raised. And I was just very comfortable me being *me*. And that's okay. I know what I'm not and so I think that my dad was comforted by that and he also couldn't believe that God could make a mistake. That was his big thing: "I can't believe that God would intentionally screw up something. So if this is true, then this must be the way that God intended it."

Hillary validated her father's search for a biological root to her lesbianism and embraced it as her own, which was a strategy common to many of the respondents in this study. A common pattern among the respondents was a desire to retrospectively create narratives of childhood differences that justified a genetic explanation for their lesbianism. Similarly, Kristin Esterberg (1997, p. 43) found that many of the lesbian and bisexual women in her study provided coming-out narratives that focused on their feelings of difference:

> The feeling of being different is probably one of the most often-mentioned cues to a lesbian or gay identity. While most people, lesbian or not, probably think of themselves as different or unique in one way or another, lesbians and bisexual women are likely to interpret that feeling of difference as evidence of a lesbian or bisexual identity. Sometimes that feeling of difference is expressed as an awareness that one is gender discrepant: liking boys' games and toys instead of girls', being a tomboy.

Like the women in Esterberg's sample, Hillary and other respondents in the current study frequently mentioned their feelings of difference when they were growing up. Retrospective accounts of differences are a pivotal aspect of coming-out models that help explain sexual identity formation. Coming-out models encourage those who are grappling with their sexual identity to formulate stories that will support or validate the slow emergence of their homosexuality. For example, Hannah explained,

HANNAH: Growing up, I was a tomboy. I preferred being called a boy to a girl. Mostly because I could do sports and that. And I just happened to like athletic things.

Tyler also differentiated her behavior as a young girl from typical "little girl" behaviors. Although she says this didn't make her a tomboy, she believed her behavior made her stand out from other little girls her age.

Similarly, Katie explained how her own adolescent athleticism became a problem for her after she married her husband. She had always played sports and did things outside with her brothers when she was young. This trend continued when she began dating her husband. However, after her children were born, her participation in athletic activities was disrupted by the expectations and responsibilities of motherhood.

KATIE: That was the big frustration; that was the big thing about being a parent. I loved my kids [. . . but . . .] I remember, my oldest son because there's eight and a half years difference between my two sons, I remember that was a major, major frustration and that was a major dilemma: how could I be *me* and be a mom at the same time? Because a mom stays in the house and they cook and clean and they prepare the kids and they are the wife and there isn't a whole lot of stuff going on outside the house. But, all the time that I was growing up as a kid, I was outside playing football with my brothers. My mother would always shoo me outside the house to go out and play and that. And it was uncomfortable for me to be in the house. And I could never reconcile that. And it was a struggle for me to be a good wife and mother and be who I was because at that time, I was in some major denial. Because at fourteen, I was like, "Yeah, I'm probably a lesbian but I'm going to pretend I'm not." And so I kind of forgot about that for a time because I was so consumed by growing up, being a wife, being a mother, and all that. But there was that struggle: how can I be me and be a good mother and a good wife?

Katie's angst over these conflicts was one contributing factor to her growing awareness of her lesbianism and eventually led to her divorce and coming-out.

Many of the respondents interpreted their feelings of difference in childhood and adolescence as an indication of the biological roots of lesbianism. Jodie's narrative provided a stunning example of rhetoric supporting the genetic nature of lesbianism.

JODIE: So, I told my mom and my sister [that I was a lesbian] and they proceeded to inform me that they had already figured it out. [. . .] And my mom, she's a sharp lady and she was just waiting and then, once I told her, that was when she related to me about how things in my childhood now started to click for her. Because she says that she never caught me sexually experimenting with boys, like little girls do when they play house and doctor. She would always catch me with my little girlfriends and I never played this game in the ghetto called "high-go-get-it" (not "hide-go-seek"). In it, you are supposed to go hide and the boy that likes you is supposed to come and find you and you are supposed to kiss him in the dark and the whole nine yards. I would never play games like that and whenever I would play house, I would always play house with all girls because none of the boys could ever play. And then if any boy made any type of pass at me or any advance at me or anything like that, I would kick his ass! I would! Boom! I would knock him down and beat the shit out of him! [chuckling] So, my mother said all these things. Like, for one Christmas, I asked for a tool kit which I wanted because I used to build go-carts. And, she said my tom-boyishness took a different level. So, she said, "Now all these things make sense to me in a life where I used to think it was just a phase or stage and you would grow out of it." But now, she knew.

After making these comments about her daughter's childhood differences, Jodie's mother concluded that these differences were an indication that Jodie was born gay. Jodie explained her mother's response:

JODIE: And she told me, "All these years, I never would have believed that people are born gay." She always thought that was a bunch of hogwash. [Instead] she thought that people *choose* to be gay. That's just what they want to do. But, she says, "But, to see my own daughter and to see the way you have grown and I'm talking about watching you from the time that you were seven or eight, I can see that that was just your nature. That is just the way you are." And it has really changed her outlook about gay people. Now, she is one of those really proud parents who proclaim: "My daughter is a lesbian."

In another interview, Paula explained how the debate over the origins of homosexuality became the impetus for her to disclose her lesbianism to her mother.

PAULA: I was talking to my mom over Thanksgiving and we started talking about gay people and my mom said, "Do you think it's environment or something?" And I said, "No, I don't think it's environment at all." I never really said that I *was* [a lesbian], but by the time we got home, she was at the stove crying. I couldn't figure out what it was all about, so before I was supposed to go back to school, my parents came upstairs, and my dad said, "Your mom and I want to talk to you about something." "Okay." "Your mom tells me that you think you might be gay." Now, I had never been with anybody at this point and it was like, "Well, yeah, I guess so." And of course, my mom was crying and she goes, "Well, who do you think you are: the boy or the girl?" My dad goes, "Oh, my god! Oh, Mary!" And then he says, "Your mom and I just want to be sure that you know what you are doing. We don't want you to do anything that might hurt you." And my mom was crying and crying and I said, "Well, I'm okay." My mom said, "Don't you feel uncomfortable when you go to the gay bars and stuff?" And I said, "Mom, it's the place that I feel the most comfortable because everyone there is like me."

Later in the same interview, Paula vehemently criticized those who characterized lesbianism as a "choice."

PAULA: I have to laugh when people say that gay parents will produce gay children because I didn't get this way because of my gay parents! I just don't get it. I don't get the whole thing. It just frustrates the hell out of me that people think it is a choice and all. Even after reading [about the woman in the short story, The Lamp], I wondered how they could even think that she chose to be that way? [with sarcasm . . .] Yeah, I choose to live a life of ridicule and have people look at me strange. [. . .] Then you want to ask people, "So, when did you choose to be heterosexual? Did you ever choose that?"

Paula resisted thinking about her sexuality as a choice, because she feared the implications for her mothering. Critics have argued that children raised in households with gay or lesbian parents are more likely to become gay, because it is presented by their parents as a socially acceptable lifestyle choice. Paula feared this possibility and thought it might be used as ammunition against her right to parent. Consequently, she argued that homosexuality is genetic, thus making it something that was beyond her individual control.

Judith Stacey and Timothy Biblarz (2001) pointed out the irony of these accounts in their critique of the body of research about the outcomes of children raised in gay and lesbian families. The existing research about gay and lesbian parenting has been both consciously and unconsciously politically motivated to emphasize the similarities between the outcomes of children raised in lesbian-headed homes and other homes, and, as a result, their unique differences have been overlooked. According to Stacey and Biblarz (2001), one important difference often overlooked by researchers has to do with the sexual identities of the children raised by lesbian- and gay-headed families. They concluded that there may be subtle differences in the ways that lesbian and gay parents interact with their children regarding issues of sexual desire and sexual practices. They further (2001, p. 178) argued that a tentative reading of the existing data points out subtle differences that suggest that:

> . . . lesbigay parents are apt to be more sensitive to issues surrounding their children's sexual development and to injuries that children with nonconforming desires may experience, more open to discussing sexuality with their children, and more affirming of their questions about sexuality. It therefore seems likely, although this has yet to be studied, that their children will grow up better informed about and more comfortable with sexual desires and practices.

While it may be true that lesbian mothers interact with their children differently regarding issues of sexuality, it is also important to recognize that existing discourses about lesbian and gay families have a strong impact on the way that lesbian mothers approach parenting. Consequently, women like Paula have an underlying motivation for sustaining and reinforcing biological explanations for homosexuality, because these origin stories provide ammunition against critics who fear that children raised by lesbian or gay parents will be raised to be gay.

Many of the forty respondents discussed issues pertaining to their children's sexuality. Two mothers specifically mentioned that their daughters were lesbians. There was a general effort among the remaining respondents to emphasize their children's heterosexual tendencies. Paula, for example, said she and her partner, Tania, were nervous when their young daughter asked questions about same-sex couples. Tania admitted that they were "real sensitized to that" and Paula explained,

> We get real concerned about that. Real concerned. And I find myself saying "When she grows up and gets married." What if she doesn't? I'm almost biased to that regular routine. But we get real sensitive to that.

This couple was not unduly paranoid when they admitted their nervousness about their child's sexual orientation, because the myth that lesbian and gay parents will raise gay children has long been used as a weapon in social and legal discourse to discredit lesbian families (DiLapi, 1989). Therefore, many mothers who wish to gain equality dismiss this myth. By denying the possibility that they will raise gay children, they must deny the possibility that sexual orientation is a choice (i.e., socially constructed), and substantiate the idea that it is a random biological event. However, the irony is that they simultaneously live one family life (i.e., lesbian) while espousing another (i.e., heterosexual) to their children. This paradox illustrates the simultaneity of micropolitics and macropolitics, as described by Deleuze and Guattari. At one and the same moment, the respondents' desires to be true to their own needs as a lesbian family and their tendency to assume heterosexuality in their children indicated the complex ways that lines of flight intersected molar structures. The respondents lived a reality that was underscored by subtle transformations that their practices initiated; these very same practices were also constituted by the workings of power in molar structures, such as the family, gender, and the law.

The respondents were mostly unaware of the mismatch that existed between their family lives and their dreams about their children's futures, because they wove narratives that compensated for the irregularities in their stories. Other researchers (Rust, 1993) have noted that lesbian women attempt to explain their sexual identities as stable and essential despite the contradictions that emerge in their narratives. Rust (1993, p. 70) found that her respondents "retrospectively perceive changes in their sexual identities as part of a goal-oriented process of discovering and accepting this essential sexuality." The conceptualization of identity as a process is similar to a "stability narrative" (Gergen & Gergen, 1988). Stability narratives allow respondents to believe in the consistency of their self-identities, while overlooking the inconsistencies that indicate the fluidity and multiplicity of identity. Stability narratives work to conceal the lines of flight that constitute the stability afforded them through their reliance on processes of reterritorialization.

Hillary and Vicky related their coming-out stories, and, in the process, illuminated their own desire to present a consistent identity to those around them. They explained that each of them had faced great resistance from their families when they disclosed their lesbianism to them. They responded to their families' fears by constructing their own stability narratives. Hillary explained how her parents were extremely upset when she came out to them. She provided them with literature from Parents and Friends of Lesbians and Gays (PFLAG) to help them address their questions and concerns. Interestingly, they eventually accepted her sexuality as long as they could view it as something biologically based. Through the embrace of a biological explanation for their daughter's lesbianism, they reinforced what they perceived to be the stability of their daughters' identities. As the quote provided earlier in this chapter suggests, Hillary also embraced that explanation and believed that her lesbianism was part of her core identity. Like other respondents who relied on biological explanations for their lesbianism, Hillary also encouraged her parents' interpretation of lesbianism as "God's will," because it allowed her to embrace her sexuality: "And I was just very comfortable me being *me*." During the period of upheaval when Hillary and Vicky came out to their parents, they kept reiterating to their parents that they had not changed simply because they had come-out as lesbians.

VICKY: So, we tried to remain really consistent and [we continued] calling even when it was really awful and difficult to call. To still do it and still say, "This is still me. I haven't changed. This is still the way I live. These are still my hobbies. This is still what I do." So, it was hard. Very hard.

To clarify, I asked, "So, they thought that this meant you were a changed person?" Hillary replied,

HILLARY: Right, that I was a changed person. So, that was tough. Very tough. Tough to see them struggling so hard with it. It was tough to remain patient when everything you see and everything you read says that you had a lifetime to get used to it but they have only a weekend or whatever. So, patience and remaining committed to that process was difficult. Very difficult. But over the course of the years, things have improved dramatically. But I think it is also a point, there's a point where they will go and then you have to recognize that [they aren't going to go any further]. We actually struggle with that even now to some extent because we have to recognize that for parents, there's a point where their comfort level is and there's a point where they won't be comfortable. It's just a fact. They won't go beyond that point. And we just have to learn to accept that. And to respect that. And I think that is still something we struggle with: knowing where that point is.

Attempts by these lesbian moms to reassert their true self, or rebuild it to include their lesbianism, involved a progressive narrative. As Hillary and Vicky's narrative suggested, their narratives reversed others' negative perceptions of decline or divergence and emphasized their self-development and improvement. Gergen and Gergen (1988) suggest that the overall purpose of story telling is to construct a narrative that presents a stable sense of self to oneself and others around you. Through story telling, these women showed how narratives are not the act of a single, autonomous actor; rather, their performances are embedded in a sociohistorical context that relies on certain features that exist solely through a preexisting social order (Gergen & Gergen, 1988, p. 40).

The compulsion to construct stability narratives is socially validated by various "experts." Because homosexuality was defined as a medical pathology until the 1970s, lesbians are still socially encouraged to seek counseling for their "problems." Despite the limitations of the developmental model for understanding sexual identity formation, it is still a common method of relieving the guilt associated with same-sex desire. Katie, for example, explained that she "figured out" her sexual identity with the aid of a therapist. This therapist helped her construct a stability narrative that explained her coming-out through a link between her earlier childhood experiences and her current desire for women. Katie found it reprehensible that "bible-thumpers tell gay people that they really aren't gay and that they have to get into therapy and if they resolved their unresolved issues. [. . .] that they really wouldn't be gay." Katie characterized these misguided conversion attempts as

> . . . a big myth because it was in my therapy that I figured it out. Looking at my childhood issues and things like that and all of the sudden, I remembered the day that I was fourteen and realized that "Oh, my god!" And remember how I got into that.

Furthermore, when lesbianism is defined as a genetic trait rather than a choice, it is possible for respondents to conceptualize their identities as a category that is fixed and essential. They can believe that their lesbianism has always been there, but it has taken some time to emerge. For many of these women, their feelings of difference and narratives about the origins of their lesbianism provided the impetus for claims to normalcy. Their assertions of normality, however, created a tension: if all lesbian women were born with a gene that predisposed them to lesbianism, then they all have some aspect of their identities in common. But, at the same time, the respondents were firmly invested in life narratives that stressed their difference from lesbians who articulated their identities in more radical forms. Thus, the respondents normalized lesbianism, but then distanced themselves from other lesbians that they perceived to be more "radical." How can these paradoxical strategies be reconciled in their daily lives?

Gergen and Gergen (1988) argue that the stability narrative is a common response to our cultural emphasis on the stabilization of social patterns. There is a sense of multiplicity in narratives due to the vast array of experiences that compose social life. However, narratives cannot be peeled away like the layers of an onion to reveal a true self; instead, the multiplicity of selves is what constitutes our sense of self. This lack of a coherent self is disguised by the workings of power in the social world, and we therefore continue to act, think, and speak as if we contain a true self. They maintain that we continue to operate as if we have a core identity, because coherence and flexibility are highly valued traits in our culture, and people construct narratives that reflect these themes of stability and change. "One does not acquire a state of 'true self' but a potential for communicating that such a state is possessed" (Ibid., p. 36). Thus, stability and growth become central keys to our personal stability narratives. Stability narratives are an important part of our lives because

> Functioning viably in a relationship often depends on one's ability to show that one has always been the same and will continue to be so and, yet contrapuntally to show how one is continuing to improve. One must be reliable but demonstrate progress: one must be changing but maintain a stable character. Achieving such diverse ends is primarily a matter of negotiating the meaning of events in relationship to each other. Thus, with sufficient skill one and the same event may figure in both a stability and a progressive narrative. (Gergen & Gergen, 1988, pp. 36-37)

Hillary and Vicky's attempts to construct a stability narrative to explain their sexual identity origins provided the grounds for them to conclude that lesbianism is innate and genetic. Other respondents came to similar conclusions, which became a vital component of respondents' claims to normalcy. Their rationale implied that a genetic explanation for lesbianism made their sexual outcome inevitable, thus providing the grounds for an argument of naturalness. In their narratives, naturalness equaled normality. Normality then became the grounds for dismissing their difference and emphasizing their similarity. Interestingly, several contradictions were built into these assumptions. For example, a genetic explanation for lesbianism suggests that there are innate differences between lesbians and heterosexual women. This reifies the heterosexual/homosexual binary dichotomy. However, in their desire to illustrate their similarities to other women, they denied their differences, and erased their earlier attempts to differentiate themselves according to biological differences. Amidst these leaps in reason, the respondents maintained a sense of consistency about their sexual identities. A theoretical focus on their claims to normalcy would emphasize processes of reterritorialization and stability, and miss the contradictions that arose from the microprocesses that disrupted the reterritorialization processes.

Sexuality and gender are unquestionably major categories that shape our experiences and the way that we think about ourselves in everyday practices. Heterosexuality remains the hegemonic ideology, and lesbianism is juxtaposed against that assumption. However, homosexuality does not clearly mark the body like race, ethnicity, or disability. Subsequently, gays and lesbians must navigate uncertain terrain as they decide when, where, and how to disclose their sexuality. Being a lesbian and a mother further complicates this process, because ideologies about motherhood hold such powerful currency in contemporary society that they can easily obscure or be strategically employed to obscure one's lesbianism. Hannah's narrative illustrated one approach for dealing with similarity and difference as a lesbian mother. She employed various narrative strategies that allowed her difference to simply float on the surface of the larger similarities she perceived she had with others around her. In the course of her attempts to obscure her difference from others, she highlighted the tensions that emerged with her attempts.

Hannah was a divorced mother of two adult sons. She gave birth to her sons during a twelve-year marriage. Although she and her exhusband got along fine, Hannah said that she always felt like a single mom, because he could never participate in family activities due to the long and chaotic hours he worked at the bakery. She was an extremely involved mom, participating in many activities with her children as well as numerous sports teams for herself. Hannah says she began her first relationship with a woman she met on her baseball team. It was at this point that she decided to seek a divorce. She said, "I had never really thought about sexuality. Never entered the picture. Never occurred to me. And, it just happened." Hannah repeatedly emphasized how little impact her emerging lesbianism had on her sense of self or her relationships with her family and friends. Her family "didn't care" when she disclosed her lesbianism to them. Consequently, she "never felt different or odd," and she "never considered the possibility that [she] was different." She counted herself lucky for her family's support and attributed her own comfort with herself to their supportive attitudes about her lesbianism. She explained that one day she slept with men, and the next day she slept with women, but that didn't influence her self-perception: "What is different about that? It didn't change me. I was still who I was." Throughout her account of her coming-out, Hannah emphasizes how little it affected her life and how little difference it made to her self-image. Consequently, she said she never embraced her sexuality as the cornerstone of her identity: "being a lesbian is not who I am. It's not a title. It's not something that I wear."

Interestingly, Hannah's claim to "normality" was built on the centralization of heterosexuality. In other words, she thought of herself as "normal" based on the fact that she didn't act differently due to her lesbianism. Consequently, her rationale implied that those who feel differently due to their lesbianism suffer from societal stigmatism because they call attention to their difference. She posed the example of hate crime legislation. She was vehemently opposed to laws that specifically targeted hate crimes, because she said that everyone should just be treated equally. Calling attention to difference was counterproductive, according to Hannah. She explained that she volunteered for my study because she wanted others to realize that lesbianism doesn't equate with difference: "I don't mind talking about it because I like people to see that we are not any different from anybody else." To validate her claim Hannah gave several examples of how she strategically interacted with coworkers in ways that downplayed her lesbianism. She explained that her partner, Brittany, attended all work-related functions with her, although she purposely never directly disclosed the nature of their relationship to her coworkers.

> We did everything together [for office-related events], Brittany and I. We were invited to people's houses and that and it was always expected, "Bring Brittany with you." [. . .] But since nobody asked directly and I'm not one to directly say [nobody knew that we were a couple]. Because of my attitude that it's not *who* I am. So, I never hinted/I never said anything. I can talk normal. Meaning: I have kids, I was married. Okay. I can talk about those things. But, it was always "Brittany and I did this, Brittany and I did that." I was never hiding things.

Interestingly, although she said she was never "hiding things," she "never hinted" about her sexuality and purposely employed this strategy in interactions with new coworkers. Hannah explained that she "likes to let them get to know [her] first" before she provided any hints about her sexuality. To exemplify this strategy, she told a story about a man that started working at her company and became her friend. After several months working together, she hinted to him that she was a lesbian; he was completely surprised. She chuckled over his response, because it further reinforced her claim that it was of little consequence to who she really was. Furthermore, she emphasized that her strategy for interacting with others at work relied on centralizing her ability to talk about "normal things," which were basically experiences she had while she was married: "I can talk normal. Meaning: I have kids, I was married. Okay. I can talk about those things." Although she claims to be "out" at work, her silence about the subject and her emphasis on "normal" experiences from her marriage suggested a subtle avoidance of the topic. Her strategy of avoidance was constantly rationalized by her claim that she was "normal," and that her lesbianism made no difference in her life and had little bearing on who she was as a person.

> So, my personal opinion is that I'm not a negative role model for either parenthood or lesbian and I like people to know that we're not always that crazy or strange or obvious or whatever. Because we are like anybody else. [. . .] I don't think people are going to get a good idea about us or a nice feeling until some of us actually talk and till society realizes that we are no different than anybody else. And that's with anything. If you are black or yellow or Jewish or anything., you are still no different. [. . .] I am only normal or we are all normal in the fact that we all want the same thing. Mostly everyone wants a nice relationship and so on and so forth. That involves respect. And sometimes gay marriages, whether it's two males or two females, people think it's different. But don't you think we argue about bills and what color we are going to paint the front room just like anybody else? So, I think that is why "normal" is stressed. And just to stress that it is no different in my house whether it is two men or two women. And that's the part that I am more interested in people knowing. "Hey! Wow, we aren't different. Don't be afraid of

us. Don't label us." But, I'm also one that does not have a lot of issues. So, I like to talk [about my experiences] because I don't have a lot of issues. To represent someone that isn't [different].

Hannah had developed a series of strategies that allowed her a sense of security about her lesbianism. She had internalized various discourses about homosexuality that encouraged her to assimilate and develop a sense of self-confidence about her sexuality. However, amidst her security, there were signs of inconsistency that indicated the subtle movement of lines of flight within and through the processes of reterritorialization that she so clearly wanted to emulate.

The paradoxes inherent in Hannah's narrative highlighted the limitations we face as researchers if we examine lesbian motherhood narratives using only conventional conceptual models. As I have shown through several examples, the lesbian mothers in this sample relied on socially constructed discourses about sexual difference as a means of normalizing themselves. Sociohistorical changes in the ways we think about homosexuality have provided the framework for such responses. Liberal humanist interpretations of sexuality allow the respondents to construct discourses about self that stress consistency and a healthy evolution toward stability and self-fulfillment. However, Hannah's and others' narratives required a closer inspection to reveal the tiny cracks in their stability narratives. These tiny fissures cannot be explained through a model that relies on a similarity/difference dichotomy for understanding sexual desire, which focuses on the lesbian subject. Instead, we need a more sophisticated analytical tool for understanding the complexity of their experiences; one that recognizes the complexity of subjectivity and the blurred boundaries that constitute what we commonly perceive as "individuals."

Deleuze and Guattari's analytical tools help explain the various strategies of reterritorialization that sustain molar structures, while also acknowledging the importance of the lines of flight that flee from them. The women's accounts of their sexual discoveries relied heavily on the coming-out model of self-discovery and acceptance. The coming-out model, however, is not a Truth; rather, it is an unstable molar structure constituted by processes of reterritorialization. The contradictions in the respondents' narratives were examples of lines of flight that simultaneously intersected and deterritorialized those molar structures. The constant processes by which the hegemonic ideologies about sexuality were simultaneously confirmed and disrupted in these women's narratives were indicative of their becomings. As I mentioned earlier in the book, becomings constitute a nexus of lines of flight that traverse and realign molar structures. Thus, the becomings described by these women through their narratives of self-discovery appear to stabilize their identities, and situate them firmly within acceptable definitions of homosexuality. However, the fissures or contradictions inherent in their accounts indicated that their experiences of self were always in movement and were never stagnant or at rest. They were comprised of intense experiences that represented movement from one moment to another where there was no endpoint, but only a series of transformative events that constituted all experiences (Grosz, 1994a). This is not to suggest that narratives can be split into pieces to reveal the multiplicity inherent in them. Multiplicity is something more complex; it is a fluidity that can only be revealed through fleeting interconnections among different processes. The narrative excerpts that I have presented throughout this chapter are mere snapshots of already changing becomings.

The respondents' stories about their own sexual identities were woven into accounts of their children's sexual identities. I hinted at this earlier in this chapter, but I will now turn to a more full discussion of these processes in the next section.

THE SEXUALIZATION OF MOTHERHOOD: "WHEN SHE GROWS UP AND GETS MARRIED"

As I have already suggested, lesbian mothers are pressured to deny the possibility that their children will be anything except heterosexual. To admit the possibility that their children are lesbian, gay, bisexual, or transgender is to admit that their own sexual orientation may have influenced the sexual identity formation of their children. Admitting this possibility is potentially dangerous, because it fuels the fires of those who criticize lesbian and gay families. However, as Stacey and Biblarz (2001) pointed out, the possibility is strong that lesbian mothers' receptivity to sexual differences may influence their parenting in subtle ways to result in differing child sexual outcomes. The respondents' stories about their children's sexual identities are telling, for they revealed fissures that indicated the processes of deterritorialization and reterritorialization that make these outcomes a possibility. I'm not suggesting that Stacey and Biblarz are entirely correct or that those who emphasize the similarities between lesbian parents and heterosexual parents are entirely correct; instead, the lived reality of lesbian mothers' lives reflects a combination of these two processes. The lesbian parents in this study sought to emphasize their similarities through the silencing of their differences. However, their differences appeared in subtle ways throughout their parenting narratives. This was particularly evident among those families where the children were not heterosexually self-identified.

Melanie recalled a difficult time in her life when her teenage daughter, Sara, ran away from home with a friend. Melanie did not see her daughter for nearly a year, but occasionally spoke to her on the phone. During that time, Sara revealed that she ran away because she was trying to deal with her own lesbianism. When her daughter finally returned to visit, Melanie expressed dismay that Sara felt uncomfortable coming-out to her own mother, a lesbian.

MELANIE: When she came home, I said, "Why did you have to leave home to come-out to me? Your mother is a dyke! I don't get it." And she said, "Well, I was so mean to you when you told me [that you were a lesbian] that I just felt so bad." So, despite being in a household where the head of the household was a dyke and being around people all of her life that were very liberal and independent and free-thinking and accepting and nonjudgmental, as much as anyone can be, that wasn't enough. [. . .] She had a mother who would *completely* accept her sexuality 100 percent. She had grandparents who would accept it/who *did* accept it/who accepted it in me and would have certainly accepted it in my daughter and, and she was surrounded by people, both gay and straight and a diverse group by class and race, that were accepting and *still* it was too scary of a thing to do. [. . .] She had a hard time with it, though. Despite growing up in what I would describe as a pretty liberal household with a lot of diversity both because of my involvement in the arts and just my own family, she certainly had never heard anything in her home sphere that was in any way prejudicial or bigoted or anti-gay or homophobic. But that doesn't mean that she didn't get it; she got plenty of it: she got it on television, she got in on the radio, she got in movies, she got it in casual conversation that you constantly have to educate your kids and make sure that they aren't picking up things that they shouldn't be, what you would want them to think.

Melanie's interactions with her daughter illustrated their intricately interwoven becomings. Their interactions as mother and daughter were similar to Deleuze and Guattari's example of an orchid and the wasp. The orchid and the wasp illustrate how we see separate entities (i.e., a wasp and an orchid), but these two entities do not really exist except through each other.

> The orchid deterritorializes by forming an image, a tracing of a wasp; but the wasp reterritorializes on that image. The wasp is nevertheless deterritorialized, becoming a piece in the orchid's reproductive apparatus. But it reterritorializes the orchid by transporting its pollen. Wasp and orchid, as heterogeneous elements, form a rhizome. It could be said that the orchid imitates the wasp, reproducing its image in a signifying fashion (mimesis, mimicry, lure, etc.). But this is true only on the level of the strata—a parallelism between two strata such that a plant organization on one imitates an animal organization on the other. At the same time, something else entirely is going on: not imitation at all but a capture of code, surplus value of code, an increase in valence, a veritable becoming, a becoming-wasp of the orchid and a becoming-orchid of the wasp. Each of these becomings brings about the deterritorialization of one term and the reterritorialization of the other; the two becomings interlink and form relays in a circulation of intensities pushing the deterritorialization ever further. There is neither imitation nor resemblance, only an exploding of two heterogeneous series on the line of flight composed by a common rhizome that can no longer be attributed to or subjugated by anything signifying. (Deleuze & Guattari, 1987, p. 10)

The orchid and wasp form a symbiotic relationship with one another: the wasp becomes-orchid, and the orchid becomes-wasp. The orchid/wasp relationship illustrates the simultaneity and interconnectedness of movements of deterritorialization and reterritorialization. Similarly, Melanie and her daughter performed a "dance" of sorts through their interactions that resembled the symbiotic relationship between the orchid and the wasp. Melanie and her daughter are both lesbians—a fact that her daughter found difficult to reveal to her mother, despite the fact that Melanie had tried to be very open-minded and liberal in her parenting. In their commonality, they were both drawn to one another and also at odds.

Academic, cultural, medical, and legal discourses of lesbian motherhood have defined the connection between lesbian parenting and their children's sexual outcomes as problematic if it results in homosexual offspring. Interestingly, many of the respondents hoped that their children *would* mature as healthy heterosexuals. To ignore the obvious connections between mothers and their children is to ignore the rhizomic nature of their familial relationships. It is inevitable that mothers and their children will influence one another in complex and unpredictable movements of deterritorialization and reterritorialization. Melanie and Sara illustrated the inevitability of this interrelationship and showed the boundless nature of rhizomic relationships. Neither mothers nor daughters are bounded, independent entities; instead, they are becomings that result from the intensities of lines and flows of their interrelationship. It is not that Sara is mimicking her mother in her lesbianism; it is "not imitation at all but a capture of code, surplus value of code, an increase in valence, a veritable becoming," a becoming-daughter of Melanie and a becoming-mother of Sara (Deleuze and Guattari, 1987, p. 10). Melanie's and Sara's ongoing attempts to grapple with these lines and flows demonstrated the instability of becomings and the constant reordering that occurs as a result of these instabilities. These rhizomic interconnections were exemplified in other respondents' stories.

Hester's story was one of heartbreak and strained relationships. Hester was the mother of five children born during a twelve-year marriage with their father. She questioned her sexuality at the time of her marriage, but remained with him for a decade before coming-out to him about her lesbianism. They were living in Florida at the time. Her husband was hurt and enraged, taking her to court for sole custody of their children based on her lesbianism. Despite the intensely conservative legal atmosphere in Florida, Hester found a sympathetic family judge who ruled in her favor. While raising her children, Hester developed several cohabiting relationships with women. She said those were often difficult breakups, because her children became attached to the other woman and the woman's children. A year ago, she met a woman online. They visited one another several times and fell in love. On one occasion, her girlfriend arrived for a visit in Florida, but appeared "different." Hester says that she knew her girlfriend was pregnant right away. Her suspicions were confirmed a month later when she called and emotionally revealed her affair with a man and begged Hester's forgiveness. Hester says that her "mothering and nurturing" personality compelled her to move to Augustia to help with the upcoming birth. Her teenage children were extremely angry. She said, "It was a situation where we almost had to put them in the car with the police out" because they were so vehemently opposed to the move. After moving to Augustia, Hester became a stay-at-home mother to her partner's baby son, during which time she became extremely attached to him.

> I was home with him from the time that [he was born]. I was in the delivery room, helped her deliver the baby. From the time that he was born to the time she moved out, I stayed home with him and she went back to work so he actually considered me his mommy. And still does! It has been very hard. Very hard. Because there have been times when she's upset with me that she keeps him away from me for a month or two. And there's nothing I can do. There's no legal paperwork that I can do to change that.

Hester's relationships with her biological children were tumultuous. She and her eldest son rarely communicated with one another. Her relationships with her other children were strained. She went through a particularly difficult time with one of her daughters. Hester's twenty-year-old daughter came-out first as bisexual, but has since come to self-identify as lesbian. Like Melanie's daughter, Hester's daughter also had a very difficult time disclosing her sexuality to her mother. Hester described years of upheaval in their family, during which her daughter was suicidal, self-mutilating, and anorexic. Eventually her daughter came to her and said, "Mom, I think I have come to a realization." Hester responded,

HESTER: "That's great. Are you saying that you are gay or are you bi?" And at first, she said, "Well, I think I'm bi. I still like guys a little." And as days, months, years went on, she's kind of more pushing guys away and getting to the point where she just wants to be around women. And to me, that's okay. I've accepted all my children just the way they are and that's the way that I think life should be.

This study was never intended to focus on the outcomes of children raised by lesbian parents. However, any discussion of parental experiences by lesbian women inevitably touches upon these issues. Lesbian parenting is particularly illustrative, because their parenting experiences are already under scrutiny before their children ever come to express their own sexual preferences. Stacey and Biblarz (2001, p. 176) suggest that potential differences in childhood outcomes among these children "are not causal, but are indirect effects of parental gender or selection effects associated with heterosexist social conditions under which lesbigay-parent families currently live." The narratives of the mothers in this study highlighted the negotiations employed as they located their own experiences within these heterosexist social conditions. Heterosexist social conditions reinforce molar ideologies about motherhood and family. However, at the same time, the lesbian mothers' parental strategies deployed various lines of flight that disrupted the stability of heterosexist social conditions. Consequently, these mothers' parental strategies for dealing with their children's sexual and gender identities were particularly illustrative of the possible lines of disruption intersecting molar heterosexist social conditions.

Kris, for example, explained how she tried to be very open-minded about her children's sexuality so she wasn't all that surprised when her daughter began "exploring."

KRIS: Hallie had her first really strong romantic attachment with another girl but has since/that relationship really decided her that she is heterosexual. I mean, she really loved that girl: they were really close, they are still really good friends. But, that is not who she is. And it was very clear to her from that experience that that was the case. And she was able to talk to me about that and, you know, when she was in the process of trying to break up with this girl and really hurting/she hadn't told me yet that they were a couple, but how stupid do you have to be! She started crying and I said, "Hallie, if this is not right for you and whether you are gay or just exploring or whatever, it's just as wrong as you to be with her if it's not right for you as it was for me to be with your dad. So you need to be honest with her and tell her how you feel. You don't have to be mean about it. Just like you would break up with a boy. Just lovingly let her know that this is not right for you." And it was hard at first because her girlfriend didn't let go for a while and there was a lot of pushing and pulling but as it turned out, that girl went to college that year and it gave them a little time apart and now they are really good friends again and everything's fine. But anyways, that experience helped Hallie to be more/she's just more open and accepting and my other daughter, Sally, has never, to my knowledge, experimented with girls, but I think that sometimes she sort of overcompensates: she is *ragingly* heterosexual to prove that she is not. There was a point where I wondered about her sexuality. At this point, I think she is probably heterosexual, but I think she has had to prove it to herself. I think that is probably true of a lot of kids of gay parents: that they feel more the need to really *prove* their sexuality.

Kris's own sexual orientation sensitized her to the nonheterosexual possibilities available to her daughters. Whereas a heterosexual mother may have not been attuned to the sexual undercurrents between Hallie and her girlfriend, Kris recognized it as a sign of sexual experimentation and encouraged her daughter to respond appropriately. Deleuze and Guattari (1987, p. 9) explain that

> Every rhizome contains lines of segmentarity according to which it is stratified, territorialized, organized, signified, attributed, etc., as well as lines of deterritorialization down which it constantly flees. There is a rupture in the rhizome whenever segmentary lines explode into a line of flight, but the line of flight is part of the rhizome. These lines always tie back to one another.

Because heterosexism dominates our cultural view and forms the molar organizations that make up family relationships, Kris's willingness to consider alternative sexual outcomes for her daughter demonstrated an instance where a line of flight flees those molar organizations. However, Kris did not have just one daughter; her other daughter, Sally, resisted the ruptures associated with alternative considerations of her sexuality and, according to Kris, reacted "ragingly heterosexual to prove that she is not [a lesbian]." Consequently, Kris's parenting took on multiple lines and flows to allow the proliferation of the multiplicities associated with each of her daughter's becomings. This is inevitable; despite the fact that molar lines associated with mothering insist that only one outcome (i.e., heterosexuality) is possible for all children. The interactions between Kris and her two daughters illustrated complex interconnections between movements of deterritorialization and reterritorialization.

Molar lines resist ruptures and seek stability. Consequently, many of the respondents related stories of others who opposed the lines of flight that disrupted those molar lines. For example, Michelle proudly encouraged her daughter to explore her boundaries. She explained how this affected her parenting and sometimes conflicted with her exhusband's parenting philosophies. Michelle's parenting philosophy extended to her expectations about her daughter's sexuality as she matured. Because her exhusband stifled their daughter's creativity in daily life, Michelle worried that he might also be judgmental if their daughter did not turn out to be heterosexual. Consequently, Michelle acknowledged that, although she would be accepting of her daughter no matter what her sexual preference, she suspected life would be easier for her daughter if she was heterosexual.

MICHELLE: Well, it would certainly be easier for her. I hope that she grows up what she feels. But it's easier to be straight because her decisions would be more well-defined. And if she's not straight, then I hope that she is comfortable with herself and she is strong enough/and I hope that Mathew teaches her that it is okay. Because it would be really hard if she came out to me and then Mathew responded badly/what do you do?

Other respondents resisted any indication that their children might be lesbian or gay. These respondents themselves resisted processes of deterritorialization. For couples like Paula and Tania, lines of flight suggesting alternative sexual outcomes for their children were threatening. The couple explained how their young daughter often played house, and there was always a mom and a dad in her make-believe family. They asked her about it and she replied,

TANIA: "I'm just playing." And I said something about why there was a father and she said, "Mom, there's all different kinds of families." Like I was the one that needed to have that explained to me. One day when we were driving in the car, she said, "Mom, can two girls get married?" And we were like, "Oh, my God! Here it comes!." So, when she asked that, both of us looked at each other like oh-my-God, here it comes. And we said, "Well, no, not really honey. Why do you ask?" And she goes, "Well, I wanted to marry my blanket." [laughing] Here we were thinking, "Oh, my God!" and here's this really simple thing: she wanted to marry her blanket and her blanket is a girl.

Paula then explained that they worried when their daughter said things that indicated she might not be heterosexual:

PAULA: We do get paranoid about things like when she says she doesn't like boys.

TANIA: We're real sensitized to that.

PAULA: Yeah. It makes us real [. . .] We get real concerned about that. Real concerned. And I find myself saying "when she grows up and gets married." What if she doesn't? I'm almost biased to that whole/that regular routine. But we get real sensitive to that.

The "regular routine" of heterosexuality described by Paula and Tania is an assumption built on the reterritorialization of molar ideologies of family life. They stifled the emergence of lines of flight that always-already existed due to their unique experiences as lesbian mothers. Consequently, Paula and Tania's parenting strategies differed significantly from those employed by Michelle and Kris.

Lucille and Becky's story about their children's sexual outcomes further illustrates my point. Lucille and Becky explained how they would never be in the annual pride parade in Augustia with their young sons because they didn't want to "expose" them to certain articulations of gay and lesbian identity.

LUCILLE: We were more politically active [before we became parents], but because we are so busy with the kids we don't have time for that. But I know for myself, I don't feel that that's really fair to your kids.

BECKY: We're not radical people. I think that when we were politically active/

LUCILLE: We weren't radical, but we were more politically active. We were more willing to go to all the marches and things like that.

BECKY: But we wouldn't put the kids into that/

LUCILLE: That's not their choice. We would do it for ourselves, but I get kind of upset when people take their little kids to the rallies/

BECKY: And put t-shirts on them.

INTERVIEWER: So you didn't go to the pride parade?

LUCILLE: *We* might go to the pride parade, but I don't believe we would take our children.

BECKY: I would take them to *see* it, but I wouldn't take them to be in it.

Lucille then explained that they felt it was important for them to participate in gay and lesbian events, even when they involved more radical gays and lesbians, so that their sons would be prepared to handle questions about their family when they got older.

LUCILLE: They're children. That's a conscious choice that you as an adult make and there's so *much* around that just to place them in that atmosphere and in the parade, I wouldn't. Yes, just to watch it. And we have talked about going back to P[rovince]town. We haven't been there in years. Because we feel that our sons need to *see* that side of our culture because we need to open up conversation and dialogue with that. What does it mean to be that radical? Why do people do that? And it's important because they are children of gay parents. They will have to discuss those things with people as they get older because people will have questions for them and we want them to be able to discuss it well and to know.

Lucille and Becky's story illustrated their (unsuccessful) attempts to avoid instigating lines of flight and the impossibility of their avoidance strategies. No matter how hard Lucille and Becky attempted to disassociate their own sexuality from their parenting, they discovered that it was impossible for them to "fit" neatly into the molar categories that they valorized. Thus, they never fully reterritorialized. Although they resisted these conclusions, they also recognized their inevitability, and instigated strategies that allowed deterritorialization to occur, such as taking their sons to the pride parade. Consequently, their becomings were interwoven with their sons' becomings in ways that explicitly relied more on molar lines than the parenting strategies employed by Melanie, Michelle, and Kris. Lucille and Becky's parenting philosophy clearly developed in response to the homophobia they experienced in their own lives and also in response to worries expressed about lesbian parenting in mainstream society. As I pointed out earlier in the previous chapter, one common myth about the children of lesbian mothers is that they will be emotionally damaged due to the stigma associated with their families. Lucille and Becky clearly wanted to prepare their sons to deal with any potential stigma they might experience as they matured. Interestingly, respondents who attempted to shield their children admitted that they would prefer that their children matured into heterosexual adults so that they wouldn't experience the stigma that they had experienced when coming-out. However, at the same time, these mothers recognized the importance of educating their children about diversity (as Lucille's narrative illustrates). This left them in a bind: they were faced with the important task of encouraging open-mindedness in their children, while, at the same time, hoping that their children were not gay. To avoid facing this paradox, most of the respondents focused on the positive outcome: that they teach their children to be open-minded and value diversity. However, their strategies for doing so differed. The differences between Victoria's narrative and Hillary and Vicky's narratives further exemplified how similar strategies can be articulated in very different ways.

Victoria was a single lesbian mother who had her son under tragic circumstances, when she was raped by a member of her family and gave birth at the tender age of sixteen. Despite the tragic circumstances of her pregnancy, Victoria had an extremely positive outlook about life; an extremely close relationship with her son, Mel; and a warm relationship with her family. She claimed that her family's influence throughout her life compelled her to raise her son to value diversity.

VICTORIA: It's a lot of the stories that I have heard from women that all the sudden have decided that they have found their sexuality and decided that they weren't happy in life. But I guess that I learned really young that you better be happy now because life is short. And if you waste thirty years just getting by then [you'll regret it]/and I think that is good because I have passed onto my son and he is the love of my life. We are best friends. We are buddies. My family has been very accepting. [. . .] I guess that I was very fortunate. We were not raised in a racist or bigoted environment and we were taught to accept people for how they are, so, I just feel that I am real lucky and I think that I have passed that along to Mel through my parenting.

In contrast to Lucille and Becky who attempted to simultaneously shield and expose their sons to difference, Victoria embraced a parenting strategy that implicitly wove her sexuality into her interrelationships with her son. She valorized her approach and criticized others who deny the connection between their families and their sexualities.

VICTORIA: I've always raised my child by myself. I guess I think of myself as a mom more than anything else and then I'm a lesbian second. It's always been a close race between the two and a balancing act between the two like it is between work: who you are in every sense of the word and trying to balance that. [. . .] I guess I'm fortunate because I never had to grapple with the issue of am I lesbian or am I straight. I never had to grapple with that. I was gay and there was no problem with it. I never had to grapple with it so I guess my identity was solid and I think that my son, because I was happy with it, then he was happy with it. I wasn't grappling with any kind of identity problem so he wasn't. If gay was okay with my mom, then it was okay with him. And he wasn't raised to think it was any different. Some parents tell their kids, "We're gay and everyone else is straight and there's a difference between the two." I've always told him, "We all pay the bills. We all go to work. We all need someone to curl up with at night because we are social creatures." It just depends on how you feel inside as to how that works out. But we are all human and we are all going to need the same things. So, he never thought it was different. [. . .]

Victoria then commented on the concerns other lesbian moms have about the impact of their lesbianism on their parenting.

> They worry about how's my son or daughter going to get into school and they have to deal with their mom being gay. Well, if you don't make an issue out of it, they won't. If you are comfortable with it, then they are comfortable with it because your children pick up on your anxieties. [. . .] If you handle it well, then your child will handle it well. I have handled it well. My son handles it wonderfully. He has been picked on: "Your mother eats pussy." All kinds of bad things. He says, "Yeah, she gets more than you do. Leave me alone!" I mean, he deals with it and moves on. He looks at people as if to say, "Is this all you have to bitch about?" So, that's how kids work. It sounds kind of goofy, but it's true.

Victoria believed that her own self-confidence about her lesbianism enabled her to convey confidence to her son so that he could deal with negative societal reactions.

> If you deal with it like "get a life" then they will deal with it, but if you are all upset about and you worry about it, then they are going to worry about it because your kids sense that. I never had a problem with it. It was always "yeah, get a life."

Like other respondents, Victoria stressed the normality of her everyday life and its similarity to other families.

> I pay my bills, I go to work, my kid goes to school, you know—there's nothing different about my household than your household. My wife is just my wife, and your life is that you have a husband and a wife. To me, it wasn't a big deal. And I have run across a lot of parents where it is a big deal to them and I think that is a detriment to their kids because it puts an anxiety on them that doesn't need to be there and if they were more comfortable with their sexuality, then I don't think it would be there. I have just as much of a right to be here as anyone else does. You know. And like I said, part of where that comes from is if the parent is anxious, then the kid is anxious.

Every respondent represented a different strategy for becoming. It is the uniqueness of the becoming processes that make unique subjectivities, despite the fact that most of the respondents felt that their experiences were anything but unique. Each of the moms developed their own approach to managing the impact of their lesbianism on their children's lives. However, all of them were confronting similar situations due to the strength of heterosexist ideologies surrounding motherhood and parenting. Their struggles to fit with molar structures revealed the futility of their attempts, because they always-already were incompatible with these structures. In fact, it is my contention that their unsuccessful struggles to conform to these structural expectations revealed the inherent instability of those molar structures. Ultimately, it revealed the instability of the category "lesbian mother." It also revealed how the respondents have completely different relationships to the molar structures, but they all must engage with them, because they are hegemonic in nature. Thus, the respondents located themselves strategically in relation to the molar structures with differing strategies resulting in different becomings.

Tyler and Michelle, who will be discussed in the next chapter, represented women who strategically questioned molar categories and, viewed them as problematic. In contrast, the remaining respondents saw lines of flight as dangerous. These disruptions were perceived as problematic, because they found that no matter how hard they tried to be "just like everyone else," they could never "fit" the molar categories and fully reterritorialize. Even though they wanted to reterritorialize, they were unable, because those molar ideologies just didn't fit them adequately. Consequently, their narratives featured a tug-of-war in which they were always attempting to reterritorialize and their efforts were always intersected by inevitable lines of flight. Strategies of reterritorialization were absent; the resources just didn't fit their needs and they were therefore always struggling to reterritorialize despite its impossibility. Tyler and Michelle, in contrast, embraced the lines of flight and their narratives highlighted the insufficiencies in molar structures and the very reasons that the other women were unable to reterritorialize.

The respondents described thus far instigated different types of lines forming the nexus between the individual and the social. In contrast, Tyler and Michelle (described in the following chapter) instigated lines that were more nomadic, because their strategies "are not always clearly distinguishable from the molecular line, which moves beyond given segments to destinations unknown in advance, lines of flight, mutations, even quantum leaps" (Grosz, 1994a, p. 204). Their strategies came closer to producing a process that Deleuze and Guattari call "becoming-imperceptible," which results in a process that eventually disaggregates the molar structures (Grosz, 1994a) and most clearly illustrates the concept of "becoming-woman," which is the "key to all other becomings" (Deleuze & Guattari, 1987, p. 277). Becoming-woman is an ongoing, perpetual process by which molar categories of womanhood are disaggregated, and the molar categories of feminine identity are destabilized (Grosz, 1994a). Those respondents who were more conservative in their strategic alliances pursued molar lines, the sorts of lines that create "the oppositions between sexes, classes, and races, and dividing the real into subjects and objects" (Grosz, 1994a, p. 204). Intermingled within these molar lines were the molecular lines "which form connections and relations beyond the rigidity of the molar line" (Grosz, 1994a, p. 204). I will now turn to the cases of Tyler and Michelle to further develop these ideas.

Chapter 7

Shifting Boundaries
and Interrogating Categories

I have illustrated the strategies employed by respondents as they sought to negotiate their own fit with various ideologies about motherhood, sexual identity, and family throughout this book. The overriding discourses deployed by the women appeared, in many cases, to be rather assimilationist: they emphasized their "normality" and similarities to other women. However, I deconstructed their strategies to reveal that beneath this veneer of assimilationism rest multilayered processes that contradictorily reinforced dominant ideologies about lesbian mothers, while also intersecting and disrupting them. In this chapter, I would like to focus on two women's narratives[1] that stood out as different from the other respondents due to their interrogation of assimilationism and the strategies that sustained assimilationism. I will show that these women's narratives, like the other respondents, illustrate the simultaneity of micro- and macropolitics, albeit through different discursive means.

TYLER

Tyler was the mother of a ten-year-old daughter, conceived within a heterosexual marriage. When her daughter was an infant, Tyler divorced her husband and, shortly thereafter, began a relationship with her current female partner. Tyler said that she had never really fit within conventional expectations about gender and sexuality. She

Lesbian Motherhood: Stories of Becoming
© 2007 by The Haworth Press, Inc. All rights reserved.
doi:10.1300/5922_08

described herself as tomboyish because she persistently challenged people's gender expectations for little girls:

TYLER: I have always been kind of, never really like a tomboy, but more assertive and aggressive and kind of strong. Wanting to have the same rights as the boys. At four years old, I refused to wear a shirt because the boys weren't wearing the shirts. And my mother's telling me "Well, I know you don't want to wear a shirt, but everyone else wants you to wear a shirt." [laugh] So, I remember feeling so disappointed that I had to put on a shirt, but I don't think it stayed on very long because I remember being like eight years old and still not wearing my shirt. Or twelve years old and not wearing my shirt. [laugh] People didn't like it very much! There were just a few people that didn't like it. Everyone else was like, "okay, whatever." Very accommodating. So there were just little things like that. I wanted to have the same rights as the boys and I would say really sarcastic things as a child. If someone told me I couldn't do something with the boys, I would say something vulgar, if appropriate. If I thought it really wouldn't offend the person. "Well, I didn't know I had to have a penis to do that" or something. It had nothing to do with a penis, just to make a point. Or vice-versa, like if it was a male thing and I was supposed to not do that, I would say, "Oh, I didn't know a vagina could stop you!" And I would fight with my dad about it—not *fight* with my dad, more like arguing/intellectual arguing. So, then there was that part of my identity.

Tyler's desire to disrupt conventional categories extended to her sexuality, which she realized was different from heterosexuality when she was a young girl. She explained how she didn't understand categories such as "lesbian," "straight," or "bisexual" and, consequently, she didn't see how they fit her own experiences. As Tyler described her own sexual identity, she first positioned herself as "bisexual" in her narrative. However, her positioning changed subtly through her narrative as she interrogated this category "bisexual" and found it insufficient to describe her own desires:

TYLER: In terms of my *sexual* identity, I *always* identified as bisexual. And after reading [the short story, "The Lamp"], I was trying to remember if there was ever any point that it was like "Ohh!" And the only thing that I could come up with was that when I was about eight years old and I was watching some television show and there were lesbians on it. And I said, "What does the word 'lesbian' mean?" to my mother. And she just hollered and laughed because here I am this little unusual person and she kind of told me in a real matter-of-fact way that I could not grasp. I was like "I don't understand." I couldn't understand why those people were *different* for that. Because you know how as a child, you kiss each other and all that stuff? I did it with both the boys and the girls and I just couldn't understand it. [. . .] It wasn't until my teen years/ my late teen years that I actually started using a word like bisexual. It didn't really fit anyway. Neither does lesbian. But that's a way to communicate *some* sort of meaning to somebody. But it really doesn't mean/to *me* when I express it what the stereotype of lesbian or bisexual means.

I asked her to clarify, "That makes sense, but I'd like you to say more about that. Like, what do those categories mean to you and how does that not necessarily fit who you are?"

TYLER: Lesbian, as a category. Well, to someone that hears me say the word lesbian conjures up an image of whatever I was seeing on the Donahue show which I didn't get. That wasn't who I was, so it didn't register that I am a lesbian. And still today, I think a lot of people conjure up a certain stereotypical image of what lesbian is: a negative or bisexual thing or it's a victimizing thing. Like, "Oh, the poor lesbian and people are mean to them and they have got all these problems and they want to kill themselves." And all this kind of thing. And that's really not what I mean if I say to somebody, if I use the word that *I* am lesbian or bisexual. What I'm referring to is just probably just alerting the person that I can have love interests in either sex or letting the person know that Carrie [i.e., her partner] is a female. Actually, I hardly ever use the word lesbian or bisexual. Like I will use the word "dyke" because it has more drama and effect. I use it in a real sarcastic way. Otherwise I just talk about Carrie the same way everyone else does and if it doesn't register to them, then I don't worry about it. I don't really think about it because it takes too much effort. It takes too much effort. [long pause] A category to me, from what I see and other people see, it's a different thing. It's a different stereotype.

Tyler felt that she stood outside the box in terms of assimilation into dominant categories of meaning surrounding sexuality and gender. She linked her desire to challenge boundaries with her personal "politics" as an adult.

TYLER: I use my sexuality or the orientation when I can, for effect and for drama. [. . .] This is my most recent example, which happened a few days ago. I was with a person who was a professional and we were in a meeting together with someone and the client said something like "the neighbor was a dyke" or something. And then he started talking about, "Oh, you know those dykes and them queens. That's the way they are. Before you know it, one of them is killing the other one." I was just dying and I just met him. And right after everybody left, I said, "Well, you know what? *I'm* a dyke!" And he said, "Oh, my God. Did I say anything wrong?" You know, just for effect. I could have done it in a much less dramatic way, I guess. And of course everyone else in the office, I had to tell them the story within ten minutes: "You know what he said in front of those people down there? He was telling about dykes and queens!" And the secretary [under her breath] "Does he *know*?" And I said, "Know *what*?" And she said, "About *you*?" And I said, "What, that I'm a dyke?" And everyone just cracked up because he had no clue. He could care less. It was just for drama. 'Cause with that person, I thought I needed to have some kind of point.

INTERVIEWER: So you opt to do that kind of . . . [fades]

TYLER: Yeah. That kind of drama and politics that are necessary.

INTERVIEWER: How do you think of it as "politics"? Why do you characterize it as "politics"?

TYLER: Because if it's a person that has some kind of power and can make some kind of decision and if I influence that person's opinion about something then they can take that information or if I can alter them then they might change things. Especially if the person has some power, in terms of if they are going to influence a law or influence a person's life in terms of how they are going to handle a case, then that is politics to me. It's making change, not just myself by standing and preaching, but by disseminating the . . . [laugh and fade] So, *that's* politics. *I* think that's politics!

In this particular instance, Tyler's "politics" indicated her desire to challenge people's assumptions about homosexuality. In her story, her male coworker was surprised and shocked to find that Tyler, a feminine (in the conventional sense of the word) appearing woman with long hair and a soft voice, was a "dyke." This clearly disrupted his ideological system. Gay and lesbian activists commonly employ similar confrontational strategies in order to disrupt heteronormativity. Thus, Tyler's notion of politics here is very similar to conventional meanings associated with "politics." However, her deployment of politics—in the sense that she intended to disrupt dominant categories of identity associated with sexuality—was a more complicated strategy than it first appeared. Through her embrace of the category "dyke" Tyler may, in fact, momentarily destabilized the ideological system in which her encounter was constituted. However, her strategy also forced her to embrace a category, namely "dyke," that inadequately described her desire. Her deployment of that category, consequently, restabilized or reterritorialized the very duality that she sought to disrupt through her "politics." This instance illuminates how her becoming was constituted by complex, multilayered, fluid, and ongoing processes of deterritorialization and reterritorialization.

Tyler's life philosophy translated into a system of interpersonal relationships that emphasized her need to interrogate dominant ideologies and challenge boundaries. Her parenting reflected these goals. She had a very close relationship with her young daughter, Arlene, and she glowed with pride when she described Arlene's independent and outspoken personality. Tyler surrounded herself with friends with similar life philosophies. Consequently, she believed her daughter had been exposed to positive influences that other children are lacking in life. When others questioned her mothering and feared that Tyler's daughter was being exposed to harmful influences, she replied with candor. In one particular instance, a coworker asked her if she thought that Arlene would prefer if her mother was in a "more conventional relationship." Tyler promptly asked her young daughter what she thought, and Arlene's reply was indicative of her mother's parenting philosophy.

TYLER: So, I asked her! She was like, "Conventional? What's that?" And I was like, "Well, would you prefer if I was more like other moms?" She was like, "What do you mean?" It took us a long time to actually understand the point of this. I was like "Well, you know that there's my partner and me instead of, like a man and me." And she was like "Well, that's not different." So, it was just pointless! So, I just threw my hands up. I'm not sure if that was the example that I had thought of earlier that I wanted to tell you. I don't know if that's good or bad! We'll find out when she grow up! [laugh] She couldn't/ I think she thinks of me, in some ways that she can put some tangible thing on that I'm kind of cool compared to a lot of other moms. And she not embarrassed of me like a lot of other moms because the kids/ some of her friends think that I am kind of cool. I don't know if that has anything to do with being a lesbian.

Early in the interview, Tyler described herself as "abstract," and struggled to explain her ideas to me. What was revealing about Tyler's narrative was her willingness to grapple with the fluidity of identity categories—a fluidity that other respondents struggled to deny. Unlike the majority of the women in the sample, Tyler didn't centralize her mothering outright in her narrative. In fact, her struggles to decide how she would characterize herself were insightful, because she seemed unable to clearly describe herself. Unlike the other respondents who attempted to fit themselves neatly into what another respondent called the "little boxes" that define our identities, Tyler struggled to explain herself outside those boundaries. Her struggles were indicative of the limitations of language and the way that semantics force us to embrace molar representations of ourselves that aren't necessarily adequate. As a result, Tyler's narrative came much closer to consciously deploying lines of flight that disrupt these molar categories. Her strategy contrasted with other respondents who less self-consciously deterritorialized molar structures only as a result of what first appeared to be assimilationist terms. For example, Tyler explained how she "always had a hard time bringing in the mothering part."

TYLER: I've been trying to figure this out after I read this. Because mothering is one of the most important parts of my personality and one of the most important characteristics to me. Just like being a fighter for people. But, lesbian mother really isn't a center of who I am. It doesn't really seem *that* different. So, I've been trying to connect them all, but it is kind of difficult for me.

Tyler acknowledged the importance of her mothering to her sense of self, but also revealed uncertainty about describing herself in such terms. When I asked her "how she would characterize herself," she elaborated:

TYLER: What I was talking about earlier: that type of personality, that type of kind of how I have dedicated my life to fighting for other people. And I think about my roles, which includes "mother" as the most important role, a lot because it's just time consuming and demanding. So there is always that role of "mother" at the back of your mind. Those are definitely the two. Almost seems like *two* characteristics that are put together that don't always belong together or it's kind of arbitrary . . . lesbian mother, okay. Without some other context to "lesbian mom," it doesn't really mean anything other different than "mom" or different than "lesbian." But if I had a context and a person was a lesbian mom and a certain thing was happening to them because of it or something, then lesbian mom would have meaning to me because other people are treating her that way because she is a *lesbian mom*. And they think something about her. Then it has meaning to me.

Tyler's dissatisfaction with descriptors like "mother" and "lesbian mother" reflected her lifelong inability to flawlessly fit herself into the many molar categories that structure social life. While there were times that she found it appropriate to embrace molar categories to describe her experiences, there were other times when those categories were inadequate. Her narrative revealed the contextuality of categories and their instability. Uncertainty was not unsettling to Tyler; in fact, she embraced it despite the fact that it made it difficult to describe herself to others. In many ways, Tyler exemplified the importance of focusing not merely on the dichotomous parts that make up lesbian motherhood. Her narrative revealed the importance of looking at the borders between these categories rather than the categories themselves. Tyler's reluctance to fit herself neatly into the categories that make up the oppositional stances explicit in molar categories (i.e., mother/nonmother, lesbian/straight, homosexual/heterosexual, and bisexual/straight) emphasized the border work that maintains these oppositional categories. On one hand, she committed herself to these categories when necessary to convey a particular identity to others. On the other hand, she transformed those categories by disputing their adequacy.

The narratives throughout this study have demonstrated that there are various analytically separable dimensions associated with categories such as "mother" and "lesbian"; however, these categories also are filled with complicated, shifting and sometimes contradictory meanings. The purpose of this book is to explore "mother," "lesbian," "woman," and "family" less as categories and more as ongoing, fluid dimensions of social relations and social organizations. The dismantling and concretization of the boundaries presented in this book are illustrative of the "becomings" described by Deleuze and Guattari (1987). "Becomings" are the result of the interplay of micropolitical and macropolitical processes. Tyler's "becoming," for example, is composed of her continuous interrogation of the molar categories that seek to stabilize her identity into compact boxes called "lesbian" (or "bisexual") and "mother." Her becoming elaborates the shifting, fluid process of identity that occurs at the boundaries between what seem to be concrete categories. Becomings are constant processes of shuffling and reshuffling of the molar categories that make up binary distributions. Becomings are "who" we *are*.

MICHELLE

Michelle described her life in very colorful and a typical terms. Raised as a born-again Christian, she spent almost five years as a missionary, traveling across the world preaching the gospels of conversion. When she was sixteen, she began to realize her desire for women and struggled with how that fit into her religion, which dooms homosexuals to eternal Hell. Her parents also strongly believed that homosexuality is an illness that can be "cured" through the teachings of God. When she met her (now ex-) husband (who also was a missionary for the church), she confessed to him that she thought she might be a lesbian. He promised that marriage would help cleanse her of her "problem." She reluctantly accepted his marriage proposal and was soon pregnant with their daughter. During her pregnancy, Michelle was "preaching the word of God" in South Africa. During her pregnancy, she began an affair with female missionary who was traveling with their group. When her daughter was about four months old, Michelle decided that she had to confess her lesbianism and leave her husband and the missionary. When she told her husband, he immediately kicked her out into the streets with their young daughter. She was alone, without money in South Africa, and unable to afford the return flight to the United States. Her lover helped her find a place to stay and also left the missionary. They stayed together for several months in South Africa, and then returned to the States together. However, their relationship turned physically violent and she left the woman shortly thereafter.

She raised her daughter as a single mother, except for one short relationship with a woman named Holly. At the time of our interview, Michelle had only recently finalized the lengthy and ugly divorce from her daughter's father. She was awarded custody, but her daughter regularly visited her father. Michelle's relationship with her exhusband had improved somewhat since the finalization of the divorce, but they continued to radically disagree on parenting issues.

Michelle had experience and wisdom beyond her twenty-five years, and she exuded self-confidence during the interview despite the uncertainties she was currently facing in her life. She was not college educated, but she was well-read and articulate. She was very introspective during the interview, and explained how she often expressed her thoughts and desires through art and written poetry and fiction. Michelle believed that women have a special gift of healing which has been suppressed by a patriarchal society. She also believed in "reembodiment" (in contrast to reincarnation), and envisioned her mothering role as one of spiritual guide. Through her parenting, she hoped her daughter "could discover the lesson that she has chosen to learn in her life." Her parenting philosophy was spiritually sustained by the belief that we choose which lessons we will learn prior to our birth; life is just a process of learning those lessons. Michelle had developed a very eclectic personal spirituality that encompassed various philosophies that she had been exposed to during her life. Michelle did not try to defend her sexuality or justify it within the strict confines of Christianity. Instead, she created her own spirituality that reflected her diverse views about reembodiment, her reason for being on Earth, and the necessity of realizing one's potential and inner beauty.

Similar to Tyler, Michelle expressed dissatisfaction with the categories that were available to explain her experiences. In particular, she resisted others' desire to define her merely by her motherhood.

MICHELLE: Sometimes when I talk to people, and I don't know if it's how they sort of preconceive my ability to parent like parenting is some essential/ some people think that it is the only thing and don't get me wrong, it is very important, but you know. And I always wonder why that is. I think that how I am as a person affects my view as a mother. And it's important to know where I came from: that I had abusive parents, drug using and alcoholic parents. But I think that I am here to help my daughter learn the lessons that she is supposed to learn. And finding what it is that I am here to learn from her. It means laughing with her and having fun with her believing in her. She is also a healer. Every once in a while, I will have a headache and she will come up behind me and massage my temples and tell me it will be okay and my headache will go away. And, we have that kind of relationship. It is a struggle because Mathew [i.e., her exhusband/the father of her child] doesn't understand it. He hampers it. That bothers me. But I try to tell her to try not to think that any ideas are wrong. Unless it is way out there, like something *obvious*. But, even when she colors, I hear Mathew say, "No, you have to color in the lines and this can't be that color." If she wants the sun to be a purple triangle, that is okay!

Michelle's story revealed her willingness to teach her daughter lessons about the beauty of nonconformity. Her exhusband's desire to color the sky blue and color within the lines symbolized the allure of molar categories and the strategies we use in our interactions to sustain those molar ideologies. Michelle, however, was willing to consider a purple, triangular sun. Michelle explained in her narrative about her journey to reconcile her own experiences with the inadequacies of dominant ideologies about motherhood and sexuality.

MICHELLE: . . . and that has been a huge part of figuring out who it is to be me. And to not put myself in any specific boxes. I think that they are there only for our own comfort. There is nothing that says that you have to say or act in a certain way so that everyone knows where you sit. The reason that you do it is because it threatens other people's faith. If you say, "I don't have a particular sexuality.

I go with whether my spirit is connected with the person to know if I have fallen in love or not." Then the other person is threatened because they don't have a way to define you and it's uncomfortable for them. And I think that's why we define ourselves the way we do [. . .]. And I think that as we grow, we are taught that we should all have a goal, we should all define ourselves, and that is good. And not being able to define yourself means that you don't know yourself. It's bad. But that's not the point! I think that putting the cover on a blank book is no more effective/it's *less* effective than having a book that is untitled but has its own story. So, I think that is important.

Michelle's analysis of her own experiences beautifully illustrated the power of macropolitical processes in narratives of everyday life. She recognized our cultural desire to cling to conventional categories because they offer a language by which we can better understand ourselves and relate with others. Like Tyler, Michelle also recognized the difficulty and dangers of border crossing. Her narrative acknowledged the inevitability of deterritorialization, but also the simultaneity of reterritorialization. Becoming involves the constant shifting and reshifting of one's sense of self; shifting is what constitutes our subjectivities.

Michelle wrote a poem that metaphorically illustrated her own becoming. When Michelle wrote this poem, she was grappling with her sexual desire for a man and how that fit into her own sense of her sexuality. Her struggles to understand her desire for this man exemplified several contradictory and simultaneous processes: (1) the need or compulsion we feel to fit our experiences into predefined categories; (2) the powerful nature of hegemonic ideologies that make us feel this way; (3) the ultimate inadequacy of these dominant categories of representation (i.e., lesbian) to capture our experiences; and (4) the limited nature of language to describe the lines and flows that constitute processes of deterritorialization and reterritorialization. The simultaneity of these processes was eloquently articulated in Michelle's unpublished poem titled "Shedding- The Metamorphosis":

> The leaves are changing
> the trees shake them off—almost gladly
> Another year, another Season . . .

They tumble to the ground
spinning~twirling, topsy-turvy
like a drunken aerialist
Propless, directionless,
and headed for some kind of end
Out with the old. . . .
I sit here, in the rain, on the porch,
cold and contemplative.
I fathom the shape, width, and size
of the box I have just crawled out of.
I feel strangely like an insect
who just shed its old shell
Outgrew it
Discarded it
The shell resembles ME so closely,
that even I am momentarily tricked
I move and stretch, "trying-out" my new definition
This one feels like it fits me,
but THAT'S what I thought of the other . . .
I never even knew I was outgrowing my old one,
but as I look back, I can see
how I started to explore less.
(Out of lack of energy, not desire)
My joints ache
from not having been extended to their full length
in quite some time.
It feels good to push past and through
I sit, curled in the fetal position, holding my knees,
I look at my old shape
I think of how lifeless it is
It occurs to me, that my shell, my label—my "defining
Proclamations,"
ARE NOT ME
They don't embody, or even aptly symbolize
who-I-am-as a person.
In fact the truth is,
they only keep me confined.
All the time I thought it was a vehicle,
it was really my cage

Funny how the difference of one mere footfall,
leaves us:
Huddled in the dark, unable to see that
it is locked from the inside
Or~Or~
Standing tall next to it, looking down at this
miniscule
object
of repression
Saying:
"How did I EVER fit in there!"

Michelle's poem offered insights into her own sense of becoming at the time of the interview. When she shared it with me, she explained that it reflected her inability to understand how her desire for her new boyfriend could be conjoined with her self-definition as a lesbian. The poem reflected her reliance on molar ideologies to understand her own experiences, while it also reflected her acknowledgement of the inadequacies of those meanings. Michelle's poem described how new experiences forced her to step outside the prior assumptions she made about herself. These assumptions had bound her within a certain category of experience that worked to reterritorialize her experiences, and disguise the lines and flows that intersected the meanings she attached to those experiences. Through her description of the "repressive" nature of these molar ideologies, she acknowledged the workings of power that sustain macropolitical processes of containment. Michelle's "escape" from these "boxes" provided her with the insight to understand the fluidity of her experiences.

However, the impression one receives from her poem (and its title, "Metamorphosis") is that Michelle moves from one box into another, albeit one that she felt was less repressive than the other. Herein lies the paradox of Deleuze and Guattari's notion of becoming: we can never "resist," if one is to understand resistance as a means of stepping outside power to instigate change or transformation. Instead, resistance comes from within (Foucault, 1990) and is constantly reterritorialized into seemingly stable molar ideologies. The constitution of one's subjectivity, therefore, can never be "truly" assimilationist or resistant as other lesbian motherhood scholars have suggested; instead, lesbian motherhood ideologies are paradoxical due to their simultaneous and contradictory processes of macro and micropolitics. Michelle's poem illustrated the unsettling quality of becoming, but also suggested new ways to envision social change and the role that individuals play in the ongoing constitution of macro- and microprocesses.

I turn in the next chapter to a brief discussion of the implications of becomings for political and change.

Chapter 8

Concluding Thoughts

In the preceding chapters, I analyzed forty lesbian mothers' narrative accounts using Gilles Deleuze and Felix Guattari's conceptual tools, particularly their conceptualization of subjectivity as a process of becoming. I used this method to better understand how the respondents situated themselves in relation to various ideological formations around them, and how they also simultaneously rewrote the intensities of movements that constitute molar structures. I began with an overview of the lesbian motherhood literature, which emphasizes the strengths of lesbian parenting and their similarities with other parents. The dominant questions posed in this genre of research concern the roles that lesbian mothers play in either resisting dominant generative powers that seek to oppress and silence them and/or the roles that they play in assimilating lesbian motherhood identities into conventional ideological systems pertaining to family life in the United States. I also provided an overview of some of the basic ways that legal discourses define lesbian mothers, particularly the dominant approaches that conceptualize lesbian mothers as either pioneers of legal change or assimilationists into existing legal frameworks.

Narrative excerpts from the respondents revealed how sensitized they were to discourses of normalization and the various ways that they integrated them into their own familial stories. Their narrative accounts of parenting and coming-out contributed to ideologies of normalization, which were deployed in and through academic and legal accounts of lesbian-headed families.

In Chapter 4, I explored the ideological formations that constitute popular and legal understandings of mothers, in general, and how these formations are translated to lesbian motherhood. In Chapter 5, I provided detailed examinations of the ways that the respondents managed their own identities in the midst of these discursive accounts of their experiences. Furthermore, I explored the contradictions and fissures that constituted the narrative accounts of the respondents. Specifically, I examined their narrative accounts of mothering, including their desire to disconnect their lesbianism from mothering, their critique of other mothers, their desire to normalize their own experiences, and strategies employed by women pursuing different trajectories to motherhood. By focusing on narrative excerpts from selected respondents, I demonstrated the instability of these narratives and the micro and macropolitics that emerged as a result of that instability.

I also examined (Chapter 6) links between parenting and sexual identify formation stories. Respondents' narratives simultaneously reaffirmed the ideology of stable sexual identities, while also disrupting and subverting it through stories that failed to fit neatly into the analytical categories proposed by sexual identity theories. The respondents' own accounts of the nature of their lesbianism became interwoven with their hopes, fears, and desires about their children's sexualities. These accounts illustrated the respondents' discomfort with the micropolitical lines that exposed the instability of the dominant ideologies they have about their own sexuality and its impact on their children. Understandably, these mothers feared the political backlash if their experiences failed to coincide with existing academic and legal accounts of their parenting that find few differences in sexual identity outcomes among children raised by gay and lesbian parents.

The contradictions that emerged in their narratives, therefore, were sometimes unsettling to the respondents. They responded much of the time by more firmly embracing molar categories that defined them as "just like any other parent." However, analyses revealed the need to more closely examine narrative accounts of everyday life in order to acknowledge the instability of these categories and the ways that these instabilities may contribute to subtle disruptions of firmly entrenched ideological formations about motherhood, parenting, and sexuality. In Chapter 7, Tyler and Michelle's narratives illustrated possible outcomes when respondents embraced these contradictions.

IMPLICATIONS

In general, this book is an analysis of parenting narratives, but it also implies the need to reconsider conventional notions of political change. Conventional feminist politics are modeled to overcome patriarchal domination through the deployment of subversive identities. My analysis, based on Deleuze and Guattari's work, re-envisions subjectivities as becomings, thus rendering conventional political thinking impotent. In accordance with many feminist poststructuralists, I question the viability of politics that are based on a stable, centered subject. Consequently, the "subjects" of my analysis—lesbian mothers—are called into question. Even as I continued to speak of the "lesbian mother" respondents throughout this book, I realized that such categories are only useful for linguistic convenience. It is not that I deny that "lesbian mothers" are part of a dominant, binary system of ordering, but instead, I would argue that the fixity and stability of that position is falsely unified. Undeniably, the respondents in this study represented concrete historical women, but their narratives also revealed the inadequacy of that unified category in the present and the past. In fact, this method of analysis not only disrupts the categories of study, but also disrupts the status of the researcher.

"I" embraced the status of "researcher" for this study; however, my experiences were as unstable and fluid as the respondents' experiences. Through the writing of this book, I found myself becoming through my work. On one hand, I pursued macropolitical strategies that required the accumulation of data and the presentation of that data within a conventional scientific method. At the same moment, I dismantled those molar structures through my analysis to reveal the myriad of lines and fissures that constituted the molar categories that appeared to perfectly define the respondents. I cannot escape the paradox of this methodological dilemma as a writer. Furthermore, and perhaps most importantly, it defines my becoming as a writer. Consequently, this book is not only an account of the becomings of the study respondents, but also an account of my own becoming. Writing is a process of becoming and thus, through my accounts of these women's stories, I also provide the reader with glimpses of my own rhizomic journey. Deleuze and Guattari argue that writing has "nothing to do with signifying. It has to do with surveying, mapping, even realms that are yet to come" (Deleuze & Guattari, 1987, p. 4).

This way of thinking does not imply that the lesbian mothers quoted throughout this book do not exist. Instead, I argue that they are never fully and completely constituted by the hegemonic discourses that seek to define and categorize them. While their narratives may seem reflective of the normalizing discourses encouraged in academic, legal, and popular ideological systems, the mothers are actually constituted by lines and flows that simultaneously reinscribe these molar structures and contribute to their apparent stability, while also undercutting and destabilizing them in the form of flows that make up micropolitics. There may be times where it is necessary and beneficial to anchor oneself to a stable identity; however, there is an inherent instability to that security that fractures upon articulation.

The result is an unstable, shifting coagulation of movements that appear as bodies. Bodies are what appear to us as a reality, because they are active and ongoing interactions of becomings (Colebrook, 2002, p. 142). These bodies are not merely a biological entity nor are they the articulation of an inner essence. "A Deleuzean body is an assemblage of forces or passions that solidify (in space) and consolidate (in time) within the singular configuration commonly known as an 'individual'" (Braidotti, 2000, p. 159). Bodies do not equate with subjectivity. This radically unsettles conventional feminist politics, which rely on "woman" as the foundation for political change.

Judith Butler (1990), for example, argued that feminism is flawed in its insistence upon a subject for political representation, because the subject is constituted by the very power system in which it operates. When feminism relies upon an agent that holds its own identity as woman, it immediately renders itself impotent. Herein lays the paradox of many forms of feminist politics: A multiplicity of refusals to acknowledge a universal subject emerge when feminists assume a common subject called "women" as the grounds of political representation. Thus, the limits of identity politics appear when those who make representational claims on behalf of the category "women" fail to recognize that they are contributing to the same system that constituted them as gendered subjects to begin with. Butler (1990, pp. 5-6) asked, "What sense does it make to extend representation to subjects who are constructed through the exclusion of those who fail to conform to unspoken normative requirements of the subject?"

Therefore, feminists must not only attempt to find their place in the current system of representation, but they must also concern themselves with the processes by which subjects called "women" are produced by the systems of power that constitute them. Butler's solution was to throw out all assumptions of universal subjects in order to dispose of the illusion that we may initiate political action that would unify women and emancipate them from universal systems of domination (e.g., patriarchy). Furthermore, she compelled feminists to critique the categories of identity that are engendered, naturalized, and immobilized by contemporary juridical systems: "Do the exclusionary practices that ground feminist theory in a notion of "women" as subject paradoxically undercut feminist goals to extend its claims to "representation? [. . .] Is the construction of the category of women as a coherent and stable subject an unwitting regulation and reification of gender relations?" (Butler, 1990, p. 5). In response, she believed we should "contest the very reifications of gender and identity . . . to trace the political operations that produce and conceal what qualifies as the juridical subject of feminism is precisely the task of *a feminist genealogy* of the category of women."

Queer theorists and feminists have seriously debated Butler's warnings. Such an outright challenge to conventional feminist politics calls for radical rethinking of political action and the agents of political change. If we disassemble the category "women," then who becomes the agent of social change? From where does change emerge? How does it flourish? Denise Riley (1988, pp. 112-113) argued that:

> . . . it is compatible to suggest that "women" don't exist—while maintaining a politics of "as if they existed"—since the world behaves as if they unambiguously did. So that official suppositions and conservative popular convictions will need to be countered constantly by redefinitions of "women." Such challenges to "how women are" can throw sand in the eyes of the founding categorisations and attributions, ideally disorienting them. But the risk here is always that the very iteration of the afflicted category serves, maliciously, not to undo it but to underwrite it. The intimacies between consenting to be a subject and undergoing subjection are so great that even to make demands as an opposi-

tional subject may well extend the trap, wrap it furiously around oneself. Yet this is hardly a paralyzing risk, if it's recognized.

Riley's insights coincide with the approach that I have taken throughout this book, because they follow closely with Deleuze and Guattari's recognition that subjectivities are formed interior to power relations, and that they are constituted by both molar and molecular intensities due to this interiority. Deleuze and Guattari's analytic concepts provide a language that describes the instabilities and intensities of subjectivities; their work highlights the impossibility of "the subject" and the necessity of shifting our focus to consider the constantly shifting interconnections that make up our experiences. Thus, our experiences, which are comprised merely of these intensities and flows, constitute our subjectivities. Our experiences are buffeted by various molar structures, and are always sustaining and undermining hegemonic structures through microprocesses associated with everyday life. This offers some hints as to how we should re-envision our political projects.

Instead of centering various subjectivity stances, such as "woman" or "lesbian," we should take an "antifoundational approach" to coalition building (Butler, 1990). An antifoundationalist politics utilizes the power of molar structures, such as "woman" and "lesbian," but also seeks out lines of flight that disrupt these dominant categories. An antifoundational politics is fleeting and temporary; a strategy that coagulates around a particular issue, but then diffuses once that issue has been addressed. An antifoundational approach to politics "seeks to undermine the idea that politics must be steady and localizable, untroubled by psychic conflict or internal disorder—a position, I might add, which can itself easily lead to disaffection and political factiousness (Fuss, 1989, p. 105). Elizabeth Grosz (1994a) describes a Deleuzian/Guattarian politics in similar ways:

> In short, Deleuze and Guattari's understanding of micropolitics, their affirmation of localized, concrete, nonrepresentative struggles, struggles without leaders, without hierarchical organizations, without a clear-cut program or blueprint for social change, without definitive goals and ends, confirms, and indeed, borrows from already existing forms of feminist political struggle, even if it rarely acknowledges this connection. (Grosz, 1994a, p. 193)

Furthermore, "[Deleuze and Guattari] are not demanding that we become instead of that we *be*: but rather, that feminism, or indeed any political struggle must not content itself with a final goal, a resting point, a point of stability or identity. Political struggles are by their nature endless and ever-changing" (Grosz, 1994b, p. 178). With the loss of a "subject" who has agency, we do not lose the power to disrupt the system. Agency, instead, becomes a product of discourse, otherwise understood as a capacity that flows from discursive formations. Agency becomes redefined by this discursive entity and (a reconceptualized form of) resistance is found within the discursive spaces that are open within particular historical moments.

A Deleuzian politics does not take the individual or subject as the agent of change. It is not a desire *of* man that propels politics; but, rather, desire in and of itself. According to Deleuze and Guattari, becoming-woman is the privileged starting point in all becomings. It is what makes becoming-imperceptible possible. Becoming-imperceptible is the ultimate experience of becoming for it frees us in ways that other becomings are not able to do. Becoming-woman was chosen rather than becoming-man because imperceptibility can never be achieved through the experience of man. This is not to say that men cannot reach this privileged place of becoming-woman. Instead, it suggests that man is the singular Subject that has been the center of our previous understandings of experience. It is the idea of the man subject that captures and prevents us from recognizing the potential of becoming. Man represents all that is molar or majoritarian.

> It is the very concept of man that has impeded us from thinking the active and affirmative difference of life. It is the concept of man that has both set us against a world of appearances, and devalued those appearances as "only" appearances. We need to see the world, Deleuze argues, not as some things that "we" know through perceptions, but as a plane of impersonal perceptions. Man, as the subject, has always functioned as that point of stable being or identity which somehow must come to know or perceive an outside world. (Colebrook, 2002, p. 139)

Consequently, we need to overcome the centrality of man in order to recognize and take advantage of the opportunities of becoming-woman. Becoming-woman is not about attaining the opposite of becoming-man, for this would trap us in the subject-oriented tradition of thinking. Instead, to think in terms of becoming-woman, we need to "think *other than being*" (Colebrook, 2002, p. 140, author's emphasis). Thus, becoming-woman is a way of overcoming the trap of man-as-being (Colebrook, 2002). "We could not say that there *is* an other of man. This would fall back into a logic of distinct beings; we can only become other, becoming other than being, become other than man: become-woman" (Colebrook, 2002, p. 140).

According to Deleuze and Guattari, all becomings must begin as a "becoming-woman" and move toward the ultimate "goal" of "becoming-imperceptible." These concepts have brought much criticism, particularly from feminists, but have also spurred productive debates that indicate their usefulness for re-envisioning feminist politics (see May, 1993a, 1993b; Grosz, 1994a; Braidotti, 1993a, 2003; Jardine, 1985). This book has been my contribution to this debate as I argued that we should conceptualize becoming-woman as a process of experiential change that brings with it new ways of experiencing life that avoid becoming mired in the stagnation of molar structures and processes. In other words, it is the process that is important rather than a concern with an ultimate goal or end-point: "Indeed the outcome of any Deleuzean 'becoming' is not emphasized, for becoming is a process, a line of flight between states which displaces and disorients subjects and identities. This 'betweenness' is experienced, not attained" (Flieger, 2000, p. 43).

It is this process of becoming that I hoped to have captured through the voices of the lesbian mothers in this book. These women themselves, if asked directly, would probably question whether their stories about narrative life can be depicted as a form of politics. They, undoubtedly, would point to other aspects of their life that are more conventionally political, such as attending a Pride rally or voicing their opposition to discrimination in the adoption process. I would not suggest that the respondents are always conscious of the lines and flows that make up their subjectivities and, consequently, are not often willing/able to cultivate the connections that ultimately lead to radical becomings. However, becomings still occur, and I think it is more useful to recognize that these processes occur always-already, often without conscious intent. There are, of course, those who are more attuned to the potentials inherent in disruptive lines and flows, such as Tyler and Michelle describe in Chapter 7. However, most of the women try to avoid these disruptions and seek the security of molar "unities." They embrace what they perceive as a stable identity and subjectivity, but in actuality, they are embracing a fleeting notion of self that is not always under the control of its maker:

> . . . the "being" of each woman is always temporary. An effect of subjectivication, it cannot be separated from a context and is always exceeded by becomings that can neither be completely controlled nor foretold. (Conley, 2000, p. 35)

This lack of control is unsettling because it undermines our perception of politics. Within this framework, it is not possible to gauge whether or not these "politics" will be successful, because "success" assumes an endpoint or successful finale. It is more micropolitical in that small experiential changes meld together to alter the molar categories that are constituted by those tiny explosions. In many ways, it centralizes the "politics" that occur at the microlevel, which are often unrecognized in our culture where formal mobilization is equated with politics. This makes for easy access for everyone and underscores the importance of recognizing the microchanges that occur through everyday experience and discourse.

At the theoretical level, my work ultimately questions our ability to neatly categorize practices and discourses within the binary frameworks commonly prescribed for understanding political agency and resistance to dominant fields of power. Furthermore, every subtle nuance of our everyday lives is saturated with some articulation of a localized subversion in the form of lines of flight. As the examples throughout this book illustrate, some lines of flight appear to be more disruptive to the molar categories through which they intersect. However, it is my contention that each and every one of the practices that make up lines of flight hold the potential for altering the ways that we experience life through molar categories. These varied and multiple strategies produce effects which are sometimes at odds with, or in opposition to the effects of other strategies also operating to constitute the phenomenon in question. Sometimes they even reinscribe those phenomena. The ideological formations that appear as molar categories in society tend, thus, to be complex and characterized by oppositions, contradictions and tensions that ultimately destabilize them. We can only understand "ourselves" and our experiences if we closely examine the contradictions that make up discourses of daily life. While it is not possible for us to position ourselves outside power and outside ideological formations in order to undo them or alter them, we may take advantage of small pockets of space that exist interior to these formations to allow for maneuver and manipulation in the form of lines of flight. Ultimately, though, these lines of flight are always fleeting, multiple, and incomplete. That makes our jobs as researchers ongoing as we must constantly reexamine these articulations and their consequences.

Appendix

TABLE 1. Respondents' Characteristics

Name	Race/ Ethnicity	Age	Occupation	Education	Yearly income	Partnered? How long?	Childrens' relationships, genders, ages	Marital history
Kim	White	33	Library Clerk	Bachelors	10,001-25,000	Yes, 8 years (Pearl)	2 Legal Guardian Children: Female, age 7; Female, age 9	No
Pearl	White	37	Grad Student	Masters	0-10,000	Yes, 8 years (Kim)	Partner's 2 Legal Guardian Children: Female, age 7; Female, age 9	No
Tyler	White	30	Law Advocate	Masters	10,001-25,000	Yes, 5 years	1 Bio Child: Female, age 10	Yes, 6 years.
Teresa	White	44	Student	Bachelors	25,001-50,000	Yes, 17 years (Monica)	2 Bio Children: Female, age 21; Female, age 20; Partner's bio child: Female, age 19	Yes, 6 years.
Monica	White	43	Professor	Masters	25,001-50,000	Yes, 17 years (Teresa)	1 Bio Child: Female, age 19; Partner's 2 bio children: Female, age 21; Female, age, 20	Yes, 3 years.
Melissa	White	50	Administrator	Bachelors	25,001-50,000	Yes, 1 year	3 Bio children: Female, age 28; Female, age 25; Male, age 24	Yes, 14 years
Julie	White	41	Counselor	Masters	25,001-50,000	Yes, 14 years (Miriam)	Partner's 1 Bio Child: Male, age 30	No
Miriam	White	58	Retired Teacher	Masters	10,001-25,000	Yes, 14 years (Julie)	1 Bio Child: Male, age 30	No

Lesbian Motherhood: Stories of Becoming
© 2007 by The Haworth Press, Inc. All rights reserved.
doi:10.1300/5922_10

TABLE 1 (continued)

Name	Race/Ethnicity	Age	Occupation	Education	Yearly income	Partnered? How long?	Childrens' relationships, genders, ages	Marital history
June	White	39	Computer Prgrmr.	Bachelors	50,001-75,000	Yes, 2 years	1 Bio Child: Male, age 17	Yes, 11 years
Penny	White	48	Admin. Asst.	Masters	25,001-50,000	Yes, <1 year	Partner's 3 Bio Children: Female, age 28; Female, age 25; Male, age 23	No
Wilma	White	47	Student	Associates	0-10,000	Yes, 4 years	2 Bio Children: Female, age 24; Female, age 19	Yes, 16 years
Sheila	White	39	Teacher	Masters	10,001-25,000	Yes, <1 year	1 Bio Child: Male, age 10	No
Melanie	White	45	Arts Mgmt.	Bachelors	25,001-50,000	No	1 Bio Child: Female, age 23	Yes, 1 year
Sara	White	36	Exec. Secretary	Associates	25,0001-50,000	Yes, 2 years (Belinda)	2 Bio Children: Male, age 6; Female, age 3	Yes, 9 years
Belinda	White	31	Program Coord.	Bachelors	25,001-50,000	Yes, 2 years (Sara)	Partner's 2 bio children: Male, age 6; Female, age 3	No
Paula	White	37	Administrator	Bachelors	75,000 and up	Yes, 15 years (Tania)	2 Bio AI Children: Female, age 4; Female, age 2	No
Tania	White	40	Chemical Tech.	Associates	25,001-50,000	Yes, 15 years (Paula)	2 Legally Adopted AI Children: Female, age 4; Female, age 2	No
Heidi	White	22	Machinist	High School	10,001-25,000	Yes, 1 year	1 Bio Child: Male, age <1 year	No
Lucille	White	38	Registered Nurse	Bachelors	75,000 and up	Yes, 11 years (Becky)	2 Adopted Children: Male, age 6; Male, age 2	No

Name	Race	Age	Occupation	Education	Income	Partnered	Children	
Becky	White	34	Social Worker	Masters	25,001-50,000	Yes, 11 years (Lucille)	2 Adopted Children: Male, age 6; Male, age 2	No
Doris	White	40	Admin. Asst.	Masters	10,001-25,000	Yes, 3 years (Stacie)	2 Bio Children: Female, age 13; Male, age 10	Yes, 14 years
Stacie	White	37	Retired Mechanic	Tradeschool	10,001-25,000	Yes, 3 years (Doris)	Partner's 2 Bio children: Female, age 13; Male, age 10	No
Gail	Black	41	Truant Officer	Associates	50,001-75,000	Yes, 3 years (Lateesha)	Partner's 5 Foster Children & 2 Bio Children: Male, age 4; Female, age 7; Female, age 6; Male, age 6; Male, age 13; Female, age 11	Yes, 5 years
Lateesha	Black/Hispanic	29	Phlebotomist	High School	10,001-25,000	Yes, 3 years (Gail)	5 Foster Children & 2 Bio Children: Male, age 4; Female, age 7; Female, age 6; Male, age 6; Male, age 13; Female, age 11	Yes, 5 years
Hillary	White	38	Professor	Masters	50,001-75,000	Yes, 10 years (Vicky)	2 AI Children: Female, age 3 (adopted); soon-to-be-born to partner, gender unknown	No
Vicky	White	38	Registered Nurse	Bachelors	25,001-50,000	Yes, 10 years (Hillary)	2 AI Bio Children: Female, age 3; soon-to-be-born, gender unknown	No
Marisa	White	34	Lawyer	Juris Doctorate	50,001-75,000	Yes, 4 years	1 Legal Guardian Child: Female, age 10	No
Hannah	White	50	Field Engineer	Tradeschool	25,001-50,000	No	2 Bio Children: Male, age 30; Male, age 25	Yes, 12 years

TABLE 1 *(continued)*

Name	Race/Ethnicity	Age	Occupation	Education	Yearly income	Partnered? How long?	Childrens' relationships, genders, ages	Marital history
Kris	White	45	Social Worker	Masters	25,001-50,000	Yes, 5 years (Denise)	2 Bio children: Female, age 21; Female, age 18	Yes, 17 years
Denise	White	43	Social Worker	Masters	25,001-50,000	Yes, 5 years (Kris)	Partner's 2 Biol Children: Female, No age 21; Female, age 18	No
Victoria	White	37	Accountant	Bachelors	25,001-50,000	Yes, <1 year	1 Bio Child: Male, age 21	No
Jodie	Black	40	Retired Nurse	Associates	10,001-50,000	Yes, 1 year	4 Bio Children: Male, age 20; Male, age 19; Male, age 18; Male, age 16	Yes, 12 years
Nancy	Portuguese/ Native Am.	51	Freelance Consult.	High School	25,001-50,000	Yes, 3 years	1 Bio Child: Male, age 26	Yes, 26 years
Katie	White	50	Social Worker	Masters	25,001-50,000	Yes, 4 years	2 Bio Children: Male, age 26; Male, age 17	Yes, 20 years
Hester	White	47	Bus Driver	Associates	0-10,000	No	5 Bio Children: Male, age 27; Female, age 20; Female, age 18; Female, age 16; Female, age 14	Yes, 15 years
Angela	White	33	Teacher	Masters	25,001-50,000	No	1 Bio Child: Male, age 6	Yes, 6 years
Lynn	White	62	Professor	Ph.D.	50,001-75,000	Yes, 28 years (Karissa)	2 Adopted Children: Female, age 8; Male, age 5	No
Karissa	White	50	Administrator	Masters	25,001-50,000	Yes, 28 years (Lynn)	2 Adopted Children: Female, age 8; Male, age 5	No

Notes

Introduction

1. See Poster (1992, 94) for the application of "resistance" in this sense.

Chapter 1

1. See the 2002 ACLU Lesbian and Gay Rights Project at http://www.aclu.org/images/asset_upload_file130_27496.pdf. Court decisions are constantly changing the legal landscape regarding gay and lesbian parenting. For the latest legal cases, refer to the Lambda Legal Defense and Education Fund (http://www.lambdalegal.org/cgi-bin/iowa/issues/record?record=5) and the ACLU (http://www.aclu.org/lgbt/relatedinformation_court_cases.html) [both accessed on November 28, 2006].

2. Quoted from an online publication by the Lambda Legal Defense and Education Fund (1997, 3), which is no longer available. For further information, refer to their website at http://www.lambdalegal.org/cgi-bin/iowa/issues/record?record=5.

3. See Shapiro (1999) for a brief history of second-parent adoption as well as a discussion of the limitations of second-parent adoptions. Second-parent adoption and "stranger adoption" are the only two avenues currently open to gays and lesbians wishing to become legal parents to their nonbiological children. "Stranger adoption" is typically used when a child has no biological parent and a legal "stranger" wishes to adopt him/her. Stranger adoptions are not as useful for lesbian couples wishing to gain joint custody of their children because "every state currently limits adoption to only one partner of a cohabiting couple, either by statute or by administrative policy" (Starr 1998). Couples may adopt jointly as "strangers" only if they are legally married. Because same-sex marriage is not legal in most of the United States, most American gay and lesbian couples cannot jointly adopt as "strangers." One couple in this study adopted two young boys internationally, and another couple domestically adopted their two children. In both cases, only one of the women in each couple was able to legally adopt the children. In Lucille and Becky's case, they actively hid their lesbianism from all their contacts in the foreign countries where they adopted, because they feared they would not be allowed to adopt if someone suspected the nature of their relationship. These cases of adoption are both examples of "stranger adoptions." It was only after the adoptions were formalized were Lucille and Kelly's partners able to pursue second-parent adoption.

Lesbian Motherhood: Stories of Becoming
© 2007 by The Haworth Press, Inc. All rights reserved.
doi:10.1300/5922_11

After the formalization of the second-parent process, all four women became legal parents to their respective children.

4. According to the ACLU Lesbian and Gay Rights Project (see entire publication at http://www.aclu.org/images/asset_upload_file130_27496.pdf; accessed on November 28, 2006), second parent adoptions have been approved at a state-wide level in nine states including California, Connecticut, Illinois, Indiana, Massachusetts, New Jersey, New York, Pennsylvania, and Vermont. Judges in other states have also approved second-parent adoptions for couples appearing in their courts, although second-parent adoptions have not been approved at the state-wide level.

5. In cases where the father is "unknown" there is an extended waiting period before the father is considered absent and a mother is allowed to legally erase his parental rights without his official permission. In one case in this study, a woman conceived her son during a one-night stand with a man whose name she did not know. Although she is now with a woman who would like to pursue second-parent adoption procedures, she is unable, because they are not able to locate the biological father. In another case, Hester held no hope that she would ever be able to achieve parental rights to her ex-partner's son who she had raised from birth as the primary caregiver. Hester began dating her ex-partner when the woman became pregnant. She describes how she supported her partner throughout the entire pregnancy and then became the primary caregiver as a stay-at-home mother. However, when they broke up, she did not have any legal ties to the child. This prevents her from being able to pursue visitation rights, and leaves her at the mercy of her ex-partner who has now decided to form a relationship with the biological father of her child. Hester explains her dilemma:

> A month later, she crying told me that she definitely was pregnant and me being the mothering, nurturing person, told her I would come up here, be her permanent partner, help her with delivering the baby, bond with the baby, take care of the baby. Um, and I stayed home with/I was home with him from the time that/I was in the delivery room, helped her deliver the baby. Um, from the time that he was born to the time she moved out, I stayed home with him and she went back to work so he actually considered me his mommy. And still does! It has been very hard. Very hard. Because there have been times when she's upset with me that she keeps him away from me for a month or two. And there's nothing I can do. There's no legal paperwork that I can do to change that. Oh, she's reached the point where she's now, um, seeing the daddy/the paternal/the 'sperm donor' I call him/asking him/biological father/he has visitation rights. She's changing the name, the baby's name, to reflect his name in order to include him in the inheritance. You know—those kinds of things. And, I'm just getting pushed aside. Lawyers have basically told me that there's nothing/ there's no legal options. But when I go to pick up and I tell him to give his mommy a hug and a kiss and tell her goodbye and he comes to *me* and gives me a hug and a kiss and says, "Let's go." Instead of giving it to *her.* So, she's been working really hard this past week on, "This is mommy. This is Hester." So, she's really, really trying diligently to make it clear to him

that I'm not his biological mother all the sudden. He's not quite two, he'll be two next month. He's just real excited to talk.

6. V.C. v. M.J.B. A-111, A-126 September Term 1998, SUPREME COURT OF NEW JERSEY, 163 N.J. 200; 748 A.2d 539; 2000 N.J. LEXIS 359, October 25, 1999, Argued, April 6, 2000, Decided, Certiorari Denied October 10, 2000, Reported at: 2000 U.S. LEXIS 6634.

7. Article no longer available at <http://www.altfammag.com/ari-glp.html>. Quotation appeared on page 5 of the online article.

8. Stan Baker, et al. v. State of Vermont, et al., No. 98-032, SUPREME COURT OF VERMONT, 170 Vt. 194; 744 A.2d 864; 1999 Vt. LEXIS 406 163 N.J. 200; Supreme Court of New Jersey, April, 6, 2000 163 Misc. 2d 999; N.Y. Fam. Ct. Monroe County, Jan. 6, 1994) Boyd's arguments are extremely provocative and potentially controversial, because she concludes that this bias could be overcome if the sexual orientation of *both* parents were taken into account in court cases involving lesbian and gay parents. She makes this recommendation as a means to challenge legal processes that assume it is always the responsibility of the lesbian or gay parent to shield their children from potentially homophobic responses from society. If *both* parents were held accountable for managing their child's well-being then the nexus approach would be fully neutral. In such cases, the judge would need to explore each parent's ability to help their children manage societal homophobia. In some cases where a heterosexual parent is having problems coping with homophobia him/herself, then the result might be granting custody to the gay or lesbian parent who is more able to handle the situation. This approach truly assumes that homosexuality doesn't matter; instead, the focus is on the parenting abilities of both parties. Rather than assuming that a child can escape homophobia by residing with a heterosexual parent, this approach acknowledges the pervasiveness of homophobia and grants custody to the parent best able to help his/her child cope with that homophobia.

9. From an online article published by PlanetOut News Staff entitled, "NY Co-Parent Wins Visitation" on October 20, 2000. Article can be found at http://www.planetout.com/pno/news/article.html?2000/10/20/2 [Accessed September 8, 2006]

10. Ibid.

11. "Mother fighting visitation puts children on view" by Jim Fitzgerald in *Associated Press Newswires*, 11/03/00.

12. First printed April 1999, http://www.colage.org/parents/custody_rights.html [Accessed September 8, 2006].

Chapter 3

1. This chapter is an adaptation of an earlier journal manuscript publication. See Hequembourg, A. (2007). Becoming lesbian mothers. *Journal of Homosexuality,* in press. The *Journal of Homosexuality* is published by Harrington Park Press (an imprint of Haworth Press, Inc., 10 Alice Street, Binghamton, NY 13904-1580). Article copies available from The Haworth Document Delivery Service: 1-800-HAWORTH. E-mail address: docdelivery@haworthpress.com.

Chapter 4

1. http://www.familyresearchinst.org/FRR_04_02.html Accessed November 30, 2005.

2. http://www.familyresearchinst.org/FRI_Bill_Proposal1.html. Accessed on November 30, 2005.

3. Cameron, P. & Cameron, K. (1996). Homosexual parents. *Adolescence,* 31, 757-776.

4. See http://psychology.ucdavis.edu/rainbow/html/facts_cameron.html. Accessed on November 30, 2005.

5. "We are family: Children and their gay or lesbian parents find fun and community in annual event in Provincetown" by Bella English in *The Boston Globe,* 07/29/00.

6. "Grandchild with same-sex parents needs support" by Vince Talott, *The Toronto Star,* 08/05/00.

7. I characterize Stacey and Biblarz's work as "courageous" because they recognized the dangers inherent in their literature review but still felt it was important to present their findings. In a recent article of self-reflection, Judith Stacey (2004) sums up the dangers and difficulties of doing public sociology and how it has impacted her own voice in this debate as well as her continued dedication to the pursuit of controversial family research:

> Having been too frequently seduced and abandoned, stood up, manipulated, and misunderstood by public suitors, I find myself a more jaded, wary social science spinster. I am learning to screen the character and credentials of my companions with greater care, to select reasonably safe public venues in which to meet, to negotiate the terms and limits of our encounters, and to temper my expectations about the prospects for success. Yet, if I have learned to adopt an ambivalent posture toward my public sociology prospects, nonetheless, when courted with sensitivity, I dare to continue to spin. (Stacey, 2004, p. 144)

Chapter 5

1. These narratives are similar to those articulated among Ellen Lewin's (1993) respondents in her study of lesbian motherhood. My intention is to more closely explore the implications of these narratives for the respondents' becomings, a line of inquiry that is entirely different from the one taken by Lewin.

Chapter 6

1. Another respondent, Belinda, echoed Hillary and Vicky's search for "normal" gays when she explained how she and her partner, Sara, were networking in the lesbian community to cultivate friendships with like-minded lesbians. Belinda exclaimed that they wanted to meet "normal people:" "I don't want super-dyke. I mean

relatively normal or a kazillion different things hanging off their body and orange or blue hair. Something normal that my kids can look at and say, 'Hey, they just look just like anybody else that's down the street.'" Sara tries to be diplomatic, "To be fair, every race and religion has its eccentrics and even the gay and lesbian population does to the point of the twenty million body piercings. [pause] What did you call them? Super-dykes? [laughing]" Belinda tries to answer, but Sara interjects, "To us, that's not the norm."

Chapter 7

1. Three women's stories—Tyler, Michelle and Melanie—did not 'fit' with the voices of the other respondents. In this chapter, I discuss Tyler and Michelle's stories in detail. Melanie's voice was presented in the last chapter and will not be explored in-depth in this chapter.

References

Arnup, K. (1995). *Lesbian parenting: Living with pride and prejudice.* Charlotte-town, Canada: Gynergy Books.

Bawer, B. (1993). *A place at the table: The gay individual in American society.* New York: Touchstone Books.

Belcastro, P. A., Gramlich, T., Nicholson, T., Price, J., & Wilson, R. (1993). A review of data based studies addressing the affects of homosexual parenting on children's sexual and social functioning. *Journal of Divorce & Remarriage, 20,* 105-122.

Bernstein, M. (2001). Gender transgressions and queer family law: Gender, queer family policies, and the limits of law. In M. Bernstein & R. Reimann (Eds.). *Queer families, queer politics: Challenging culture and the State* (pp. 420-446). New York: Columbia University Press.

Boyd, S. (1998). Lesbian (and gay) custody claims: What difference does difference make? *Canadian Journal of Family Law 15,* 133-152.

Braidotti, R. (1993). Discontinuous becomings: Deleuze on the becoming-woman of philosophy. *Journal of the British Society for Phenomenology 24*(1), 44-53.

Braidotti, R. (2000). Teratologies. In I. Buchanan & C. Colebrook (Eds.). *Deleuze and feminist theory* (pp. 156-172). Edinburgh: Edinburgh University Press.

Braidotti, R. (2003). Becoming woman: or sexual difference revisited. *Theory, Culture & Society, 20,* 3, 43-64.

Brown, L. S. (1995). Lesbian identities: Concepts and issues. In A. R. D'Augelli & C. J. Patterson (Eds.). *Lesbian, gay, and bisexual identities over the lifespan: Psychological perspectives* (pp. 3-23). New York: Oxford University Press.

Brown, S. & Lunt, P. (2002). A genealogy of the social identity tradition: Deleuze and Gauttari and social psychology. *British Journal of Social Psychology, 41,* 1-23.

Butler, J. (1990). *Gender trouble: Feminism and the subversion of identity.* New York: Routledge.

Butler, J. (1993). *Bodies that matter: On the discursive limits of "sex."* New York: Routledge.

Butler, J. (1997). *The psychic life of power.* Stanford: Stanford University Press.

Clunis, D. M., & Green, G. D. (1995). *The lesbian parenting book: A guide to creating families and raising children.* Seattle, Washington: Seal Press.

Colebrook, C. (2002). *Gilles Deleuze.* London: Routledge.

Conley, V. (2000). Becoming-woman now. In I. Buchanan & C. Colebrook (Eds.). *Deleuze and feminist theory* (pp. 18-37). Edinburgh: Edinburgh University Press.

Coontz, S. (1992). *The way we never were: American families and the nostalgia trap.* New York: Basic Books.

Lesbian Motherhood: Stories of Becoming
© 2007 by The Haworth Press, Inc. All rights reserved.
doi:10.1300/5922_12

Coontz, S. (1997). *The way we really are: Coming to terms with America's changing families.* New York: Basic Books.

Culhane, J. G. (1999). Uprooting the arguments against same-sex marriage. *Cardozo Law Review 20,* 1119-1226.

Dalton, H. L. (1991). Reflections on the lesbian and gay marriage debate. *Law & Sexuality 1*(1), 1-8.

Dalton, S., & Beilby, D. (2000). That's our kind of constellation: Lesbian mothers negotiate institutionalized understandings of gender within the family. *Gender & Society 14*(1), 36-61.

Deleuze, G., & Guattari, F. (1987). *A thousand plateaus: Capitalism and schizophrenia.* Minneapolis, MN: University of Minnesota Press.

DiLapi, E. M. (1989). Lesbian mothers and the motherhood hierarchy. *Journal of Homosexuality, 18,* 101-121.

DiQuinzio, P. (1999). *The impossibility of motherhood: Feminism, individualism, and the problem of mothering.* New York: Routledge.

Duclos, N. (1991). Some complicating thoughts on same-sex marriage. *Law & Sexuality 1*(31), 31-61.

Dunne, G. A. (2000). Opting into motherhood: Lesbians blurring the boundaries and transforming the meaning of parenthood and kinship. *Gender & Society 14*(1), 11-35.

Esterberg, K. (1997). *Lesbian and bisexual identities: Constructing communities, constructing selves.* Philadelphia: Temple University Press.

Ettelbrick, P. L. (1993). Who is a parent?: The need to develop a lesbian conscious family law. *NYLS Journal of Human Rights, 10,* 513-553.

Flieger, J. (2000). Becoming-woman: Deleuze, Schreber and molecular identification. In I. Buchanan & C. Colebrook (Eds.). *Deleuze and feminist theory* (pp. 38-63). Edinburgh: Edinburgh University Press.

Foucault, M. (1979). *Discipline and punish: The birth of the prison.* New York: Vintage Books.

Foucault, M. (1990). *The history of sexuality: An introduction.* New York: Vintage Books.

Fuss, D. (1989). *Essentially speaking: Feminism, nature & difference.* New York: Routledge.

Gabb, J. (2001). Desirous subjects and parental identities: Constructing a radical discourse on (lesbian) family sexuality. *Sexualities, 4,* 333-352.

Gergen, K. & Gergen M. (1988). Narrative and the self as relationship. In L. Berkowitz (Ed.), *Advances in Experimental Social Psychology* (pp. 17-56). San Diego: Academic Press, Inc.

Glenn, E. N. (1994). Social constructions of mothering: A thematic overview. In E. N. Glenn, G. Chang and L. R. Forcey (Eds.), *Mothering: Ideology, experience, and agency* (pp. 1-29). New York: Routledge.

Goldstein, J., Freud, A., & Solnit, A.J. (1973). *In the best interests of the child.* New York: Free Press.

Golombok, S., Spencer, A., & Rutter, M. (1983). Children in lesbian and single-parent households: Psychosexual and psychiatric appraisal. *Child Psychology and Psychiatry 24*(4), 551-572.

Gottman, J. S. (1990). Children of gay and lesbian parents. *Marriage and Family Review, 14,* 177-196.

Green, R. (1978). Sexual identity of 37 children raised by homosexual or transsexual parents. *American Journal of Psychiatry, 135,* 692-697.

Green, R., Mandel, J., Hotvedt, M., Gray, J., & Smith, L. (1986). Lesbian mothers and their children: A comparison with solo parent heterosexual mothers and their children. *Archives of Sexual Behavior 15*(2), 167-184.

Grosz, E. (1994a). A thousand tiny sexes: Feminism and rhizomatics. In C. V. Boundas & D. Olkowski (Eds.). *Gilles Deleuze & the theater of philosophy* (pp. 187-210). New York: Routledge.

Grosz, E. (1994b). *Volatile bodies: Toward a corporeal feminism.* Bloomington: Indiana University Press.

Harding, J. (1998). *Sex acts: Practices of femininity and masculinity.* London: Sage Publications.

Hare, J. (1994). Concerns and issues faced by families headed by lesbian couples. *Families in Society: The Journal of Contemporary Human Services 75,* 27-35.

Harris, M. B., & Turner, P. H. (1985/86). Gay and lesbian parents. *Journal of Homosexuality 12*(2), 101-113.

Hequembourg, A., & Arditi, J. (1999). Fractured resistance: The debate over assimilationism among gays and lesbians in the United States. *The Sociological Quarterly 40*(4), 663-680.

Hequembourg, A., & Farrell, M. (1999). Lesbian motherhood: Negotiating marginal-mainstream identities. *Gender & Society 13*(4), 540-557.

Hoeffer, B. (1981). Children's acquisition of sex role behavior in lesbian-mother families. *American Journal of Orthopsychiatry 51*(31), 536-543.

Hoffnung, M. (1998). Motherhood: Contemporary conflict for women. In S. Ferguson (Ed.), *Shifting the center: Understanding contemporary families* (pp. 277-291). Mountain View, CA: Mayfield Publishing Company.

Ingraham, C. (1999). *White weddings: Romancing heterosexuality in popular culture.* New York: Routledge.

Istar Lev, A. (1998). Lesbian and gay parenting. *Alternative Family Magazine.*

Jardine, A. (1985). *Gynesis: Configurations of woman and modernity.* Ithaca: Cornell University Press.

Kirkpatrick, M. (1987). Clinical implications of lesbian mothers studies. *Journal of Homosexuality 14*(1/2), 201-211.

Kirkpatrick, M., Smith, C., & Roy, R. (1981). Lesbian mothers and their children: A comparative study. *American Journal of Orthopsychiatry, 51,* 545-551.

Lewin, E. (1993). *Lesbian mothers: Accounts of gender in American culture.* Ithaca: Cornell University Press.

Lewin, E. (1995). On the outside looking in: The politics of lesbian motherhood. In F. D. Ginsburg & R. Rapp (Eds.), *Conceiving the new world order: The global politics of reproduction* (pp. 103-121). Berkeley: University of California Press.

Lewin, E. (1998). Negotiating lesbian motherhood: The dialectics of resistance and accommodation. In Susan Ferguson (Ed.), *Shifting the center: Understanding contemporary families* (pp. 322-337). Mountain View, CA: Mayfield Publishing Company.

Lott-Whitehead, L., & Tully, C. T. (1993). The family lives of lesbian mothers. *Smith College of Studies in Social Work 63*(3), 265-279.

Martin, A. (1993). *The lesbian and gay parenting handbook: Creating and raising our families.* New York: HarperPerrenial.

Martin, J. (1998). The lamp. *Alternative Family Magazine* (out of print). Last accessed on December 9, 1998 at http://www.altfammag.com/lamp.htm.

Maxwell, N. G., Mattijssen, A.A.M., & Smith, C. (2000). Legal Protection for all the children: Dutch-United States comparison of lesbian and gay parent adoptions. *Arizona Journal of International and Comparative Law 17,* 309-347.

May, T. (1993a). *Between genealogy and epistemology: Psychology, politics, and knowledge in the thought of Michel Foucault.* University Park, PA: The Pennsylvania State University Press.

May, T. (1993b). The system and its fractures: Gilles Deleuze on otherness. *Journal of the British Societies for Phenomenology 24,* 3-14.

McClennen, J. (2003). Researching gay and lesbian domestic violence: The journey of a non-LGBT researcher. *Journal of Gay & Lesbian Social Services 15*(1/2), 31-45.

Miller, J. A., Jacobsen, R. B., & Bigner, J. J. (1981). The child's home environment for lesbian vs. heterosexual mothers: A neglected area of research. *Journal of Homosexuality 7*(1), 49-56.

Nelson, F. (1996). *Lesbian motherhood: An exploration of Canadian lesbian families.* Toronto: University of Toronto Press.

Parks, C. (1998). Lesbian parenthood: A review of the literature. *American Journal of Orthopsychiatry 68,* 376-389.

Patterson, C. J. (1994). Children of the lesbian baby boom: Behavioral adjustment, self-concepts, and sex-role identity. In B. Greene & G. Herek (Eds.), *Contemporary perspectives on lesbian and gay psychology: Theory, research and applications* (pp. 156-175). Thousand Oaks, CA: Sage.

Patterson, C. J. (1995). Families of the lesbian baby boom: Parents' division of labor and children's adjustment. *Developmental Psychology 31*(1), 115-123.

Polikoff, N. D. (1982). Gender and child custody determination: Exploring the myths. *Women's Rights Law Reporter,* 183-202.

Polikoff, N. D. (1990). This child does have two mothers: Redefining parenthood to meet the needs of children in lesbian-mother and other nontraditional families. *The Georgetown Law Journal 78,* 459-575.

Polikoff, N. D. (1991). Educating judges about lesbian and gay parenting: A simulation. *Law and Sexuality 1,* 173-183.

Poplin, D. (1997). Truth? You can't handle the truth. *Gay Community News.* Summer: 6-9.

Poster, M. (1992). The question of agency: Michel De Certeau and the history of consumerism. *Diacritics 22,* 94-107.

Reimann, R. (1997). Does biology matter? Lesbian couples' transition to parenthood and their division of labor. *Qualitative Sociology, 20,* 153-185.

Riley, D. (1988). *"Am I that name?": Feminism and the category of 'women' in history.* Minneapolis: University of Minnesota.

Rivera, R. (1979). Our straight-laced judges: The legal position of homosexual parents in the United States. *The Hastings Law Journal 30,* 873-891.

Rubin, R. (Nov. 2, 2000). Who's my father? Progeny seek some conception of sperm donors. *USA Today.*

Rust, P. C. (1993). 'coming-out' in the age of social constructionism: Sexual identity formation among lesbian and bisexual women. *Gender & Society 7*(1), 50-77.

Scott, J. W. (1988). Deconstructing equality-versus-difference: Or, the uses of poststructuralist theory for feminism. *Feminist Studies 14,* 33-49.

Semetsky, I. (2003). The problematics of human subjectivity: Gilles Deleuze and the Deweyan legacy. *Studies in Philosophy and Education 22,* 211-225.

Shapiro, J. (1999). A lesbian-centered critique of second-parent adoptions. *Berkeley Women's Law Journal, 14,* 17-39.

Shore, E. A. (1996). What kind of a lesbian is a mother? *Journal of Feminist Family Therapy 8*(3), 45-62.

Skolnick, A. (1991). *Embattled paradise: The American family in an age of uncertainty.* New York: Basic Books.

Somers, M. (1994). The narrative constitution of identity: A relational and network approach. *Theory and Society 23,* 605-649.

Stacey, J. (2004). Marital suitors court social science spinsters: The unwittingly conservative effects of public sociology. *Social Problems 51*(1), 131-145.

Stacey, J., & Biblarz, T. (2001). (How) Does the sexual orientation of parents matter? *American Sociological Review 66,* 159-183.

Starr, K. (1998). Adoption by homosexuals: A look at differing state court opinions. *Arizona Law Review 40,* 1497-1514.

Stein, A. (1992). Sisters and queers: The decentering of lesbian feminism. *Socialist Review, 22,* 33-55.

Stein, A. (1997). *Sex and sensibility: Stories of a lesbian generation.* Berkeley: University of California Press.

Tasker, F., & Golombok, S. (1995). Adults raised as children in lesbian families. *American Journal of Orthopsychiatry 65*(2), 203-215.

Thorne, B. (1982). Feminist rethinking of the family: An overview. In B. Thorne & M. Yalom (Eds.). *Rethinking the family: Some feminist questions* (pp. 1-24). New York: Longman.

Thorne, B. (1995). *Gender play: Girls and boys in school.* New Brunswick, NJ: Rutgers University Press.

Victor, S. B., & Fish M. C. (1995). Lesbian mothers and their children: A review for school psychologists. *School Psychology Review 24,* 456-479.

Wald, J. (1997). Outlaw mothers. *Hastings Women's Law Journal 8*(1), 169-193.

Weedon, C. (1987). *Feminist practice & poststructuralist theory.* Oxford: Basil Blackwell.

Weston, K. (1991). *Families we choose: Lesbians, gays, kinship.* New York: Columbia University Press.

Wright, J. (1998). *Lesbian step families: An ethnography of love.* New York: Harrington Park Press.

Index

Page numbers followed by the letter "t" indicate a table.

Lesbian Motherhood: Stories of Becoming
© 2007 by The Haworth Press, Inc. All rights reserved.
doi:10.1300/5922_13